my first COOKBOOK

BY
Rena Coyle

ILLUSTRATED BY
Jerry Joyner

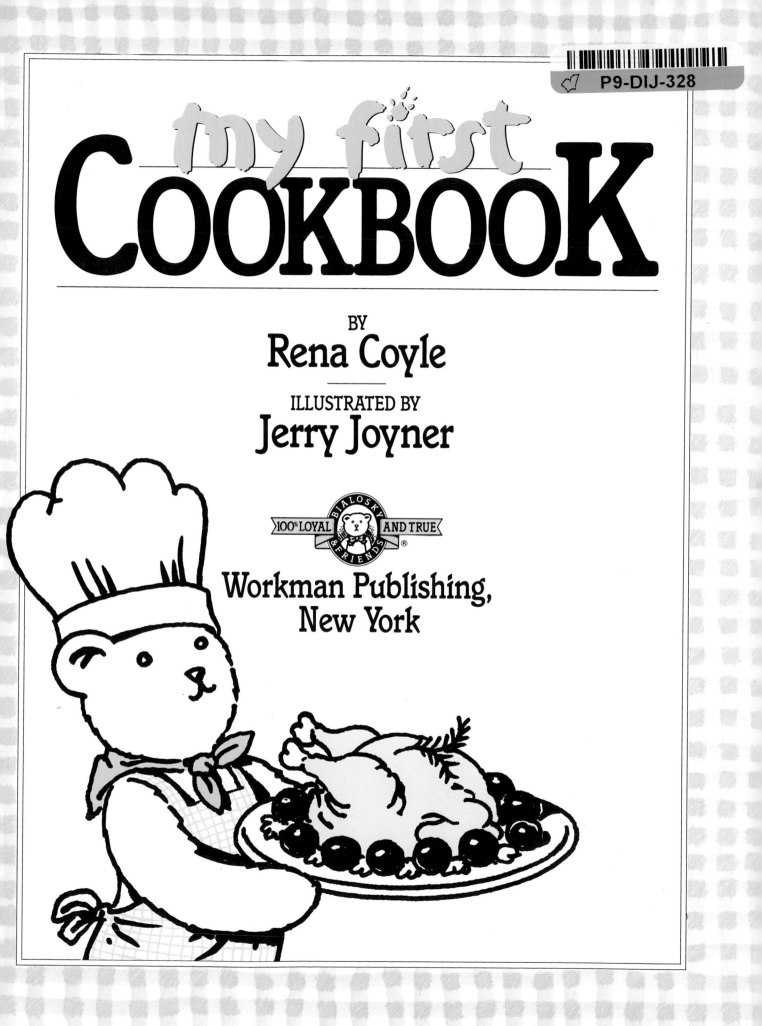

100% LOYAL BIALOSKY AND TRUE & FRIENDS

Workman Publishing,
New York

Library of Congress Cataloging-in-Publication Data
Coyle, Rena.   My first cookbook.
Includes index.
    Summary: Provides fifty recipes for breakfast, lunch,
snacks, dinner, dessert, and special occasions, with
step-by-step illustrations and serving suggestions.
Includes tips on safety and adult assistance.
1. Cookery—Juvenile literature. [1. Cookery]
I. Joyner, Jerry, ill. II. Title. III. Series.
TX652.5.C655 1985   641.5′ 123   84-40683
ISBN 0-89480-846-X

Cover and book design by Tedd Arnold
Cover illustration by Jerry Joyner

Workman Publishing Company, Inc.
708 Broadway
New York, NY 10003

Manufactured in United States of America
First printing October 1985
15   14   13   12   11   10   9   8

CONTENTS

FROM: Bialosky
TO: All my friends

Hi!
My name is Bialosky and I love to cook.

Sharing a meal with friends and family is one of the most pleasant ways to spend time together. Helping to make that meal is even more fun and is something that anybody of any age can do. Preparing food that is delicious is an exciting adventure, and rewarding—you get to bake your cake and eat it, too!

I have selected some of my favorite dishes for you to prepare at home. The sections are divided into recipes to serve at different mealtimes or at snack time, and I couldn't resist adding a couple of extra sections, in full color, that include some of my special-occasion and holiday favorites. Of course, you can eat these dishes whenever you or your family feel like it: the Egg McTeddy is great for lunch as well as breakfast; you don't have to wait for a rainy day to make the Cinnamon-Raisin Bread.

Before you begin cooking the recipes, be sure to read through the hints and safety tips. Then you'll be ready to put on your apron, roll up your sleeves, and get cooking!

Have fun,
Bialosky

GETTING STARTED

Before You Begin

1. Once you have chosen a recipe to make, ask an adult to read it through with you. You can discuss any help that you may need and make sure you understand all the different steps.

Many of the recipes call for the use of electric appliances, knives, top-of-the-stove and inside-the-stove cooking. In each of these cases, younger cooks *will need adult assistance*. Bialosky has left his paw print at the top of recipes for which we believe extra supervision is necessary. In all cases, young cooks should never begin any recipe without first consulting an adult.

2. Check to see that you have all the ingredients you will need for the recipe you've selected. If you must buy some things, make a list noting exactly how much of each item you will need. This way you won't buy too little or too much. Make sure you have all the necessary utensils, too.

3. When you are ready to begin, put on your most comfortable old clothes. You should always wear an apron when cooking, but even when you have one on, occasionally a splash or splatter will find its way onto your clothes.

4. Cooking is easier when you don't feel crowded. Start with a clean work surface and allow yourself plenty of room. It may mean asking an adult to help you clear off a counter.

5. Before handling food, wash your hands in warm soapy water, then rinse and dry them thoroughly.

Safety First

1. You will need to use a sharp knife in some of these recipes. Never pick up a knife by the blade—only by its handle. When you are ready to cut, make sure that the sharp edge is facing down, toward the ingredient that you are cutting. When you have finished using it, always lay the knife down flat on the counter.

2. When you have a pot cooking on the top of the stove, turn its handle in toward the center of the stove. This will prevent anyone from bumping into it and spilling the hot contents.

3. Always keep oven mitts and pot holders handy at the side of the stove. Remember to pick up a pot holder before lifting a hot pan from a burner. Before removing one from the oven, first put on your oven mitts.

4. When checking or removing a pan from the oven, first pull out the rack part way. Don't reach into a hot oven to get a pan. Make sure that you have either a cooling rack or a trivet nearby on which to place the hot pan. Never place a hot pan directly on the counter—it may burn the surface.

5. Whenever you need to use an electric appliance (a blender or mixer, for example), always be sure your hands are clean and *dry* before you plug it in. When you have finished preparing the recipe, be sure to unplug whatever appliances you used, again with clean, dry hands.

6. When using a blender, make sure the lid is firmly in place before you turn the machine on. This will prevent food from splattering all over the counter and the cook. Never scrape down the food inside a blender while the machine is on. Turn it off first, then wait until the blades are no longer moving before you add or stir any ingredients.

7. When using a mixer, never put your fingers into the bowl while the machine is on. If you want to taste the recipe, turn the mixer off first and make sure the blades have stopped moving before putting in a spoon or your fingers.

8. Always turn off the stove burners and oven as soon as you finish using them.

Clean Up

1. You will always be invited back into the kitchen if you leave it sparkling clean. Carefully stacking used bowls and pots in the sink as you go along makes cleaning up at the end a lot quicker. If you have to use a number of utensils to make a dish, it might be easier to clean and rinse as you go along.

2. When you have finished using an ingredient, put it back where you found it. The same holds true for kitchen utensils. Then, next time you reach for something, it will be there.

Cooking Procedures

How to Crack an Egg
1. Hold the egg in one hand and tap the middle of the shell, gently but firmly, against the rim of a bowl, until it cracks.

2. Place your thumbs along both sides of the crack and, holding the egg directly over the bowl, pull apart the shell until it separates. Let the egg slide into the bowl. If a piece of shell drops into the bowl, just ease it out with your finger. It doesn't matter if the yolk breaks unless the recipe calls for you to separate the egg yolks from the whites.

In that case, you will have to be extra careful not to pierce the yolk with your finger or with the broken edge of the shell.

Separating an Egg
Separating an egg means keeping the yolk separate from the white. You will need to do this when you make the soufflé on page 45.

1. Place a wide-mesh strainer in a mixing bowl.

2. Carefully crack and separate the eggshell as described above. Let the egg drop gently into the strainer.

3. Lift the strainer. The white will drip through the holes into the bowl and the yolk will remain in the strainer.

4. Pour the yolk into a different bowl.

Rolling Out Pastry

1. Sprinkle flour lightly on a clean kitchen counter or pastry board and on a rolling pin.

2. Place the dough in the center of the space and using the heel of your hand, flatten it slightly.

3. Place the rolling pin in the center of the dough and firmly roll it away from you.

4. Lift the dough and turn it a quarter turn. Place the rolling pin in the center and again firmly roll it away from you. Repeat this process of turning and rolling until the pastry is the size you want it to be. If the dough begins to stick, sprinkle a little more flour on the rolling pin and the counter. If the dough splits too much around the edges, gather up the dough into a ball and begin again. (Try not to do this too many times, because it will change the texture and flavor of the final pastry.)

How to Knead Dough

In order for dough to be well blended, you must knead it. To knead dough, sprinkle flour lightly on a clean kitchen counter. Place the dough on the counter. Place the heels of your hands in the center of the dough. Firmly push the dough away from you from the center out, stretching it as far as you can. Then take the edge you just pushed away and fold it over the other half of the dough. Pick up the dough, turn it a quarter turn, and begin the pushing and stretching again. If the dough gets sticky, sprinkle the counter with a little more flour. Keep up the kneading for the amount of time given in the recipe. Your dough should look shiny and well blended when you are finished.

How to Punch Down Dough

When you make a yeast bread, you have to allow time for the yeast to fill the dough with air two or three times before you finally bake the bread. To get the air out of the dough between risings, you have to punch down the dough.

Remove the dough from the bowl it has been resting in and place it on a counter. Using your fist, punch the dough several times until all the extra air has escaped—sort of like letting the air out of a balloon.

BREAKFAST

Egg McTeddy

FULL-TIME ADULT · ASSISTANT NEEDED

Layer all the best breakfast ingredients on an English muffin—and create an Egg McTeddy. On very special occasions, prepare this dish using croissants or stuffed inside a brioche.

1 Using the largest holes on the grater, carefully grate the cheese over a sheet of waxed paper. (Do this slowly, so you don't scrape your knuckles.) You should have about ½ cup. Tear the ham slices into small pieces, or if the slices are too thick to tear, carefully cut the ham into small pieces on the cutting board with the utility knife. Pick off tiny sprigs of the fresh dill or measure out the dried dill.

2 Break the eggs into the small mixing bowl and beat with the fork until the yolks and whites are well blended.

Ingredients

2 ounces Cheddar cheese (about ½ cup grated)

4 ounces sliced cooked ham (about 6 thin slices)

1 sprig fresh dill or ¼ teaspoon dried dill weed

6 eggs

4 English muffins

3 tablespoons butter, at room temperature

—————

Makes: 4 servings

Utensils

Grater

Waxed paper

Measuring cups

Cutting board

Utility knife (optional)

Measuring spoons

Small mixing bowl

Fork

Toaster

Table knife

Frying pan

Wooden spoon

Pot holder

Preparation time: 15 minutes

Cooking time: 10 minutes

3 Using the fork, pierce the edges of the English muffins and gently pull the halves apart. Toast the muffins in the toaster, then butter the rough side of all the muffins, using 2 tablespoons of the butter.

4 Melt the remaining 1 tablespoon butter in the frying pan over medium heat. Pour the beaten eggs into the frying pan and stir with the wooden spoon. When the eggs begin to stick, sprinkle in the cheese, ham, and dill. Cook, stirring gently, until the eggs are firm but not dry.

5 Spoon the eggs on the 4 muffin bottoms. Cover with the muffin tops and serve immediately.

Tip If you are using croissants instead of muffins, you will need to split them in half with a utility knife. Do it slowly because croissants are a little fragile and you don't want them flaking into a million pieces.

Teddy Bear Pancakes

Be an artist and create your next batch of pancakes in the shapes of Teddy Bears. These directions include the easiest design, but you can make your bears look any way you'd like.

Ingredients

4 tablespoons (½ stick) butter

½ cup all-purpose flour

½ cup whole-wheat flour

1 ½ teaspoons baking powder

½ teaspoon sugar

¼ teaspoon salt

1 egg

1 cup milk

Applesauce (optional)

Honey (optional)

Makes: 20 pancakes

Preparation time: 20 minutes

Cooking time: 20 minutes

Utensils

Large frying pan

Pot holder

Measuring cups

Measuring spoons

Large mixing bowl

Wooden spoon

Small mixing bowl

Whisk

Spatula

Ovenproof plate

Oven mitts

1 Heat 2 tablespoons of the butter in the frying pan over medium heat until it melts. Remove the pan from the heat and set it aside.

2 Place the all-purpose and whole-wheat flours, baking powder, sugar, and salt in the large mixing bowl and stir it together with the wooden spoon.

3 Break the egg into the small mixing bowl. Add the melted butter and the milk and whisk together very well.

4 Pour the egg mixture into the flour mixture and whisk until the batter is quite smooth and has almost no lumps.

5 Preheat the oven to 200°F.

6 Melt a quarter of the remaining butter in the frying pan over medium heat. Holding the handle of the pan with a pot holder, tilt the pan so that the melted butter coats the bottom evenly.

7 To make a Teddy Bear pancake, spoon 1 tablespoon of the batter into the pan for the body and then add 1 teaspoon above the body for the head. With another teaspoon of the batter, make the ears, hands, and feet. Make as many pancakes as will fit in the pan without touching.

8 Cook the pancakes over medium heat until you can see bubbles on top, about 2 minutes; then lift up one edge of a pancake with the spatula and look to see if the bottom is golden brown. If it is brown, flip it over and cook until the second side is golden brown, about 2 more minutes.

9 Remove the cooked pancakes from the pan, place them on the oven-proof plate, and set the plate in the oven to keep the pancakes warm until you are ready to eat.

10 Melt more butter in the pan as needed and make more pancakes until the batter is gone.

11 When you are ready to serve, put on the oven mitts and remove the plate from the oven.

Tip These pancakes are delicious served with applesauce that has been sweetened with a touch of honey.

Did You Know?
Pancakes are also known as flapjacks, griddlecakes, and hotcakes, and in one part of the United States are called "Rocky Mountain Deadshots!"

Sausage Pockets

You can prepare these pockets ahead of time and freeze them, so that they will be ready to cook up for a special breakfast treat. About 45 minutes before breakfast, place the frozen sausage pockets on a cookie sheet and bake them in an oven preheated to 400°F.

Ingredients

2½ cups all-purpose flour

2½ teaspoons baking powder

1 teaspoon salt

4 tablespoons (½ stick) butter, at room temperature

⅔ cup milk

2 ounces Cheddar cheese (about ½ cup grated)

1 egg

1 tablespoon water

8 breakfast sausage links

Makes: 8 sausage pockets

Preparation time: 15 minutes

Baking time: 25 minutes

Utensils

Measuring cups

Measuring spoons

Large mixing bowl

Wooden spoon

Rolling pin

Ruler

4-inch cookie cutter or widemouthed glass

Grater

Waxed paper

Small mixing bowl

Fork

Pastry brush (optional)

Cookie sheet

Oven mitts

1 Preheat the oven to 400°F.

2 Place 2 cups of the flour, the baking powder, and the salt in the large mixing bowl and stir it together with the wooden spoon.

3 Add the butter. Using your fingers, rub the butter with the flour until the butter disappears into the flour. It is all right if a few small lumps of butter are left.

4 Pour in the milk and stir until the dough is thick and blended.

5 Sprinkle a third of the remaining flour onto a clean kitchen surface. Using your hands, scoop out the dough from the bowl onto the floured surface and flatten it with your hands. Sprinkle some more flour over the dough and brush it evenly over the top with your hand. Brush off any extra flour. Using the rolling pin, roll the dough out until it is about ¼ inch thick (page 8). Use a ruler to measure if you aren't sure.

6 Using the cookie cutter, cut as many circles from the dough as you can. Remove the extra dough from around the circles and form the scraps into a ball. Flatten the scraps, sprinkle a little more flour on them, roll them out, and cut out as many more circles as you need to make 8.

7 Using the largest holes of the grater, carefully grate the cheese onto a piece of waxed paper. (Do this slowly, so you don't scrape your knuckles.) You should have about ½ cup.

8 Break the egg into the small mixing bowl and add the water. Gently beat with the fork until well mixed. With the tip of your finger or with a pastry brush, dab the egg around the edge of each circle.

9 Place 1 sausage link in the center of each circle and sprinkle the cheese over the sausages. Fold the dough circles over the sausages and press the edges together with your fingers to seal the sausages inside.

10 Place the sausage pockets on the cookie sheet. Brush the tops with the egg wash to give them a shine. Put on the oven mitts and place the cookie sheet in the oven. Bake for 25 minutes.

11 Look to see if the tops of the biscuits are golden brown. If they aren't ready, bake them a little longer, checking them every 2 minutes. When they are ready, put the oven mitts on and remove the cookie sheet to a heat-proof surface. Let them cool for 10 minutes before eating.

Oatmeal with Fresh Pear Sauce

FULL-TIME ADULT · ASSISTANT NEEDED

An old breakfast favorite tastes deliciously like hot granola when served up with chunky sweetened pears, raisins, and crunchy walnuts. Great on cold winter mornings.

Ingredients

3 cups water

2 tablespoons brown sugar

¼ teaspoon salt

1⅓ cups quick-cooking oatmeal

2 ripe pears

3 tablespoons raisins

3 tablespoons chopped walnuts

2 cups milk (optional)

Makes: Four ½-cup servings

Utensils

Measuring cups

Medium-size saucepan with lid

Pot holder

Measuring spoons

Wooden spoon

Apple corer

Vegetable peeler

Blender or food processor

Preparation time: 10 minutes

Cooking time: 5 minutes

1 Measure the water into the saucepan. Set it on the stove and heat the water to a boil over medium heat. Add 1 tablespoon of the brown sugar and the salt to the boiling water. Add the oatmeal and stir it into the water with the wooden spoon. Heat again to a boil and cook, stirring occasionally, for 2 minutes. Turn the heat off, put the lid on the pan, and let it sit for 5 minutes.

2 Place the pears on a counter. Push the corer through the center of each pear, twist the core out of the pear, and discard. Peel the pears with the peeler.

3 Break the pears up with your hands and place the pieces in the blender or food processor. Add the remaining 1 tablespoon brown sugar. Turn the blender or processor on and process the pears to a chunky sauce.

4 Divide the oatmeal evenly into 4 cereal bowls and spoon some pear sauce over each serving. Sprinkle the raisins and nuts over the sauce and serve. You can serve the oatmeal with a pitcher of milk.

Did You Know?

The Pennsylvania Dutch word for dried fruits like raisins is snits.

SPECIAL OCCASIONS

BREAKFAST IN BED

There are all kinds of reasons to treat someone to a breakfast-in-bed surprise: it's their birthday or anniversary; it's Mother's or Father's Day; or even as a treat for a great report card. Sweet and crunchy granola-stuffed apples make these special occasions stand out even more. They go nicely with cold milk or Dreamy Hot Chocolate (page 76).

BAKED STUFFED APPLES

Ingredients

4 medium-size apples
⅔ cup granola
¼ cup chopped walnuts
2 tablespoons wheat germ
2 tablespoons honey
½ cup apple cider
1 cup vanilla yogurt

Makes: 4 stuffed apples

Utensils

Apple corer
Measuring cups
Measuring spoons
Large mixing bowl
Wooden spoon
8- or 9-inch square baking pan
Aluminum foil
Oven mitts
Fork or skewer
Large serving spoon

Preparation time: 15 minutes

Baking time: 45 minutes

1 Preheat the oven to 350°F.

2 Press the corer through the center of each apple and twist out the

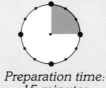

core (it makes a hole that is about ¾ inch wide). The hole should go through the entire apple.

3 Place the granola, walnuts, wheat germ, and honey in the large mixing bowl and stir it all together. Using your hands, fill each apple hole with the granola filling. Top the apples with any extra filling.

4 Place the apples in the baking pan and pour the cider around the apples.

5 Cover the pan with aluminum foil and seal the edges by folding the foil tightly around the rim.

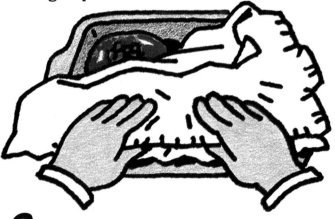

6 Put the oven mitts on and place the pan in the oven. Bake for 45 minutes. Then put the oven mitts on and carefully open one end of the foil. Pierce one of the apples with the fork or skewer. If the fork slides in easily, the apples are done. If the apples are still hard, reseal the foil and bake for another 15 minutes. When the apples are ready, put the oven mitts on and place the pan on a heatproof surface.

7 Carefully remove the foil, opening the edge that is away from you first to let the trapped steam escape. Using the large spoon, scoop the apples out of the pan and set them on a serving plate. Spoon any cider syrup in the bottom of the pan over the apples. Top each apple with 3 tablespoons of the yogurt. The apples are best served warm.

Tip These apples can be prepared the night before and baked when you get up in the morning. Just cover them with plastic wrap and put them in the refrigerator.

Did You Know?
There are over 3,000 named varieties of apples today.

RAINY DAY BAKE-OFF

FULL-TIME ADULT
• ASSISTANT NEEDED •

When you're stuck indoors with nothing special to do, why not bake this delicious bread? You'll have plenty of time to let the loaves rise and when the baking is finished, the reward is fragrant slices to smear with cream cheese and enjoy with Mulled Apple Cider (page 73).

CINNAMON-RAISIN BREAD

Ingredients

2 cups milk

1 package active dry yeast

5 to 6 cups all-purpose flour

¾ cup sugar

2 teaspoons salt

½ cup (1 stick) butter, at room temperature

1 tablespoon oil

2 teaspoons ground cinnamon

¼ cup raisins

Cream cheese (optional)

Makes: 2 loaves

Utensils

Measuring cups

Small saucepan

Measuring spoons

Large mixing bowl

Wooden spoon

Kitchen towel

Paper towels

2 loaf pans, each 8 x 4 inches

Small mixing bowl

Utility knife

Pastry brush

Oven mitts

Cooling rack

Baking time: 35 minutes

Preparation time: 3 hours

1 Pour the milk into the saucepan and place it on the stove. Heat the milk over medium heat until it steams and you can see tiny bubbles around the edge of the pan. Turn off the heat and let the milk cool for 10 minutes.

2 Place the yeast, 5 cups flour, ½ cup of sugar, and salt into the large mixing bowl and stir it all together with the wooden spoon. Add 2 tablespoons of the butter and the milk. Stir until it forms a stiff dough. If it isn't stiff, add another ¼ cup flour.

3 Sprinkle a clean working surface lightly with flour. With your hands move the dough from the bowl to the floured surface. Sprinkle a little more flour over the top of the dough.

4 To knead, first press the dough flat with your fingers. Place the heels of your hands on the dough, press them down, and push the dough away from you.

Curl your fingers over the far edge of the dough and fold it back over itself.

Turn the dough a quarter turn.

Push and then fold the dough in half again. Continue to turn, push, and fold the dough for 5 minutes. If the dough starts to stick, sprinkle a little more flour under and over it. Shape the dough into a ball.

5 Wash out the mixing bowl and dry it. Pour the oil into the bowl and spread it all over the bottom and side of the bowl with a paper towel. Put the dough in the bowl and then turn it over so that the top is oiled. Cover the bowl with the kitchen towel. Place the bowl in a warm place that isn't drafty and let it rise until the dough is twice as big as it was, about 1 hour.

6 Remove the dough from the bowl and punch it down with your hands. It will look like a balloon with the air just let out. Shape the dough into a ball again and put it back in the bowl. Replace the towel and let it rise for 30 minutes.

7 Use a paper towel to rub 1 tablespoon of the butter on the bottoms and sides of the loaf pans.

8 Place 4 tablespoons of the butter, the remaining ¼ cup sugar, and the cinnamon in the small mixing bowl and stir it all together.

9 When the dough has risen the second time, sprinkle a large clean surface lightly with flour and move the dough from the bowl to the floured surface. Using your hands, flatten the dough and shape it into a rectangle as thin as you can make it.

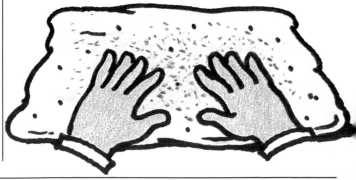

10 Also with your hands, spread the butter mixture over the surface of the dough and then sprinkle the raisins over the dough. Wash your hands.

11 Starting at one long edge, roll the dough up as tightly as you can. Using the utility knife, cut the dough in half to make 2 loaves and place each loaf in a buttered pan seam side down. Cover the pans with the towel and let the loaves rise in a warm place for 30 minutes.

12 Preheat the oven to 350°F.

13 Using a pastry brush, spread the remaining 1 tablespoon butter over the tops of the loaves. Put the oven mitts on and place the pans in the oven. Bake until the tops are golden and the bread sounds hollow if you lightly tap it with a knuckle, about 35 minutes.

14 Put the oven mitts on and place the pans on a heatproof surface. Put one of the pans on the cooling rack and tip it over on its side. Let the bread slip out. Do the same with the other pan. Let the bread cool on the rack.

Tip Serve cream cheese to smear on thickly cut slices of Cinnamon-Raisin Bread. The combination will be a sure-fire hit.

TV TRAY TREAT

When you have friends over for some after-school television watching, these fruit sticks make easy-to-eat snacks. You can get them ready before your favorite show starts and take them out of the fridge during a commercial break.

FRUIT ON A STICK

Ingredients

2 apples
1 banana
10 grapes
10 strawberries
2 tangerines
1 cup vanilla yogurt
¼ cup shredded coconut

Makes: 6 servings

Preparation time: 25 minutes

Utensils

Paper towels
Cutting board
Apple corer
Utility knife
Wooden cocktail skewers
Small mixing bowl
Wooden spoon
Serving plate

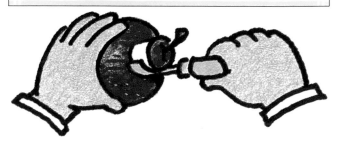

1 Rinse the apples and dry them with a paper towel. Place the apples on the cutting board. Push the apple corer through the center of each apple and twist out the core (it makes a hole that is about ¾ inch wide). Using the utility knife, cut the apples in half. Place each half flat side down on the cutting board, cut the halves into thick slices and then cut across the slices to make bite-size chunks.

2 Peel the banana and cut it into bite-size slices.

3 Rinse the grapes and strawberries and pat them dry. Pick the green hulls off the strawberries.

4 Peel the tangerines and separate the fruit into segments. Remove as many seeds as you can.

5 Carefully push the fruit in any order you like onto the pointed ends of the skewers. Put all the skewers on a serving plate.

6 Pour the yogurt into the mixing bowl, add the shredded coconut, and mix it together with the spoon. You can dip the fruit into the yogurt or spoon a little over each stick.

HAPPY BIRTHDAY

Mini-chocolate chips help to make this cake special. Bake one for your best friend or your brother or sister on their birthday. The frosting is so good it will be hard to keep from eating it instead of spreading it on the cake. Just keep telling yourself that you can lick the bowl!

FROSTED CHIPPER CAKE

FULL-TIME ADULT ASSISTANT NEEDED

Ingredients

1 cup (2 sticks) plus 2 teaspoons butter, at room temperature

4 cups plus 2 tablespoons flour

1 ¾ teaspoons baking soda

½ cup packed dark brown sugar

⅓ cup granulated sugar

3 eggs

3 ¼ cups sour cream

⅓ cup orange juice

3 cups mini-chocolate chips (1 ½ twelve-ounce bags)

Chocolate Frosting (recipe follows)

¼ cup chopped walnuts

Tube of prepared cake decorating gel (optional)

Makes: 10 servings

Utensils

Paper towels

12- x 9-inch cake pan

Measuring spoons

Measuring cups

Medium-size mixing bowl

Fork

Large mixing bowl

Electric mixer

Rubber spatula

Oven mitts

Cooling rack

Cookie sheet

Birthday candles

Candle holders

Preparation time: 30 minutes

Baking time: 1 hour and 15 minutes

1 Using a paper towel, rub the 2 teaspoons of butter on the bottom and sides of the cake pan. Add the 2 tablespoons of flour to the pan and slowly turn and shake the pan to coat the inside evenly with flour. Turn the pan upside down over the sink and shake out the excess flour.

2 Preheat the oven to 350°F.

3 Place 4 cups flour and the baking soda in the medium-size mixing bowl and mix it with the fork.

4 Place 1 cup butter and the brown and granulated sugars in the large mixing bowl. Using the electric mixer, beat the butter and sugars at high speed until they are light and very creamy, about 3 minutes. Stop when necessary to scrape down the side of the bowl with the rubber spatula.

5 Break one of the eggs into the bowl and beat until the egg is completely mixed in. Add the last 2 eggs and beat again until blended.

6 Add half the flour mixture and mix it in at low speed. Add 1¾ cups of the sour cream and mix at low speed. Add the remaining flour and mix. Then add the remaining sour cream and mix. Add the orange juice and mix again. To make this easier, you can turn the mixer off while you add each new ingredient. Add the chocolate chips and mix at the lowest speed until the chips are evenly distributed throughout the batter.

7 Using the rubber spatula, scrape the batter into the baking pan. Smooth the top with the spatula so that the batter is spread evenly in the pan.

8 Put the oven mitts on and place the pan on a rack in the center of the oven. Bake for 1 hour and 15 minutes. Put the oven mitts on and pull out the rack a little way so that you can see the cake. If the cake has shrunk slightly from the sides of the pan, it is ready. If it hasn't, bake 10 minutes longer and check again.

9 When the cake is ready, place the cooling rack on top of the cake pan. Turn the pan upside down and gently let the cake fall onto the cooling rack. Carefully pull the pan straight up and off the cake. Let the cake cool while you make the frosting.

10 When the cake is cool, turn it right side up onto a cookie sheet. Frost the cake by taking a big scoop (about half) of the frosting with the spatula and placing it on top of the cake. Spread the frosting evenly over the top. Scoop up a small amount of the frosting remaining in the bowl and spread it evenly along the sides of the cake. Continue scooping and spreading until the cake is completely frosted.

11 Sprinkle the cake with the chopped nuts. Place birthday candles in their holders around the edges in a pretty pattern and let the celebration begin.

Tip If you would like to put a birthday message on the cake, first write it out on a piece of paper. When you are sure it is right, copy it onto the cake using the cake decorating gel.

Chocolate Frosting

Ingredients

1 ½ cups confectioners' sugar

¼ cup cocoa powder

½ cup (1 stick) butter, at room temperature

1 package (8 ounces) cream cheese, at room temperature

1 teaspoon vanilla extract

Makes: 1 ¾ cups

Preparation time: 20 minutes

Utensils

Strainer

Soupspoon

2 large mixing bowls

Measuring cups

Electric mixer

Measuring spoons

Rubber spatula

1 Place the strainer in one of the mixing bowls. Pour the confectioners' sugar and cocoa powder into the strainer. Gently shake the strainer from side to side, sifting the mixture into the bowl. Press through any lumps left in the strainer.

2 Place the butter and cream cheese in the other mixing bowl. Turn the electric mixer to a low speed and blend the butter and cream cheese together. When they are blended, turn the mixer off. Measure ¼ cup of the cocoa and sugar mixture and add that to the butter and cream cheese. Turn the mixer back on at low speed and carefully blend the two mixtures. Add the remaining cocoa and sugar mixture, ¼ cup at a time, until it has all been blended into the butter and cream cheese.

3 Add the vanilla extract to the frosting mixture. Turn the mixer on low and blend in the vanilla until it all disappears into the mixture. Turn off the mixer and unplug it.

4 When the mixer blades have stopped turning, use your fingers to clean the blades of extra frosting. Scrape it into the bowl (or your mouth). Use the spatula to scrape down the sides of the bowl so that all the frosting is piled in the center of the bowl.

TEA PARTY

Scones are traditional English teatime biscuits. This variation, preferred at Teddy Bear teas, uses milk rather than cream, and honey rather than sugar. Serve the scones with butter and more honey—naturally!

CINNAMON-HONEY SCONES

Ingredients

1 ¾ cups all-purpose flour

1 ½ teaspoons baking powder

¼ teaspoon ground cinnamon

6 tablespoons (¾ stick) butter, at room temperature

1 tablespoon honey

½ cup milk

1 egg

Butter for serving (optional)

Honey for serving (optional)

Makes: 8 scones

Utensils

Cookie sheet

Aluminum foil

Measuring cups

Measuring spoons

Medium mixing bowl

Wooden spoon

Large soupspoon

Oven mitts

Cooling rack

Spatula

Preparation time: 20 minutes

Baking time: 15 minutes

1 Preheat the oven to 450°F.

2 Line the cookie sheet with a piece of aluminum foil.

3 Place the flour, baking powder, and cinnamon in the mixing bowl and stir to mix with the wooden spoon.

4 Add the butter to the flour mixture and work it into the flour with your hands. The butter will disappear into the flour and the flour will look somewhat yellow.

5 Add the honey and milk and then break the egg into the bowl. Stir with the wooden spoon until thoroughly mixed.

6 Using the soupspoon, scoop up a spoonful of dough and drop it onto the lined cookie sheet. Leaving room between each spoonful, continue until there's no more dough in the bowl.

7 Put the oven mitts on and place the cookie sheet on a rack in the center of the oven. Bake for 15 minutes. Then look to see if the scones are golden. If they aren't, bake for another 2 minutes and check again. When they're ready, put the oven mitts on and place the cookie sheet on the cooling rack.

8 Let the scones cool for about 5 minutes; then slide the spatula under each scone and place them in a basket or on a serving plate. Scones are best when they are eaten warm.

Fruit Tea

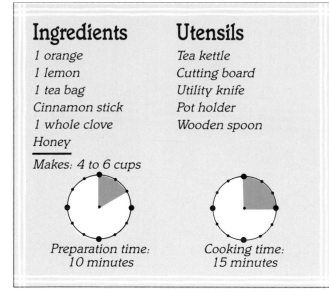

Here is a perfect tea to accompany freshly baked scones.

Ingredients
1 orange
1 lemon
1 tea bag
Cinnamon stick
1 whole clove
Honey

Makes: 4 to 6 cups

Utensils
Tea kettle
Cutting board
Utility knife
Pot holder
Wooden spoon

Preparation time:
10 minutes

Cooking time:
15 minutes

1 Fill a kettle with at least 6 cups of cold tap water. Place it on the stove and bring the water to a boil over medium-high heat.

2 Place the orange on the cutting board, and using the utility knife, cut it into 4 quarters. Remove as many seeds as possible and put 2 of the quarters in a teapot. Set the remaining quarters aside.

3 Place the lemon on the cutting board, and using the utility knife, cut it into 4 quarters. Remove as many seeds as possible and put 2 of the quarters in the teapot. Set the remaining quarters aside.

4 Add the tea bag, cinnamon stick, and clove to the teapot.

5 When the water boils, ask an adult assistant to help you remove the kettle from the stove. Pour the boiling water into the teapot. Cover the pot and let the mixture heat for 3 minutes. Remove the cover and using the wooden spoon, press down on the orange and lemon quarters. Give the tea a good stir, then remove the tea bag and the other ingredients with the spoon.

6 Carefully fill 4 tea cups with the freshly brewed tea. Serve with honey and the extra orange and lemon quarters. Let friends sweeten and flavor their tea to taste.

LUNCH

Sandwich Bread Box

The pimiento- and cucumber-spread sandwiches will surprise your friends and family because they are different and so tasty. But you can fill the bread box with any of your favorites, like peanut butter and honey or tuna or egg salad.

Ingredients

1 large round loaf of bread, unsliced

12 thin slices whole-wheat bread

1 cup Cucumber Sandwich Filling (recipe follows)

12 thin slices white bread

1 cup Pimiento Sandwich Filling (recipe follows)

Polar Bear Pickles (recipe follows)

Makes: 12 sandwiches

Preparation time: 40 minutes

Utensils

Cutting board

Long bread knife

Utility knife

Table knife

Piece of ribbon, 30 inches long

1 Place the loaf of bread on the cutting board. With an adult's help and using the bread knife, carefully cut a 1½-inch-thick slice from the top of the loaf. Using the tip of the utility knife, cut a circle around the inside of the bread, trying not to cut through the bottom of the loaf. Using your hands, remove the insides of the loaf, leaving a thick shell of crust. Save the bread to feed the birds or ducks. Set the shell and top aside while you make the sandwiches.

2 Place the whole-wheat bread on the cutting board. Using the utility knife, carefully trim the crusts from the bread. Save these crusts for the birds, too. Spread the cucumber filling evenly over 6 slices of the bread and top with the remaining 6 slices. Using the utility knife, carefully cut the sandwiches diagonally in half.

3 Place the white bread on the cutting board and trim the crusts as you did the whole-wheat bread. Spread the pimiento filling evenly over 6 slices of the bread and top with the remaining 6 slices. Cut the sandwiches diagonally in half.

4 Put all the sandwiches in the bread box. It's okay if they stick up above the edge of the box. Place the top on the bread box. Wrap the ribbon around it and tie in a bow on top. Serve with the crisp pickle spears.

Tip Bread boxes can be made in all sizes and shapes. Larger loaves will hide more sandwiches, but if only one or two friends are visiting, you can buy a smaller loaf. Just remember that the box needs to be made from a bread that is unsliced.

Cucumber Sandwich Filling

Ingredients

1 large cucumber
1 teaspoon salt
1 small onion
1 package (8 ounces) cream cheese, at room temperature

Makes: 1½ cups, enough for 6 sandwiches

Utensils

Vegetable peeler
Cutting board
Utility knife
Teaspoon
2 medium-size mixing bowls
Measuring spoons
Wooden spoon
Strainer
Paper towels
Small bowl
Plastic wrap

Preparation time: 30 minutes

1 Using the peeler, peel the skin from the cucumber. Place the cucumber on the cutting board and carefully cut the cucumber lengthwise in half, using the utility knife.

2 Holding one of the halves in your hand, insert the teaspoon under the seeds and scoop the seeds out. Throw the seeds away. Seed the other half of the cucumber the same way.

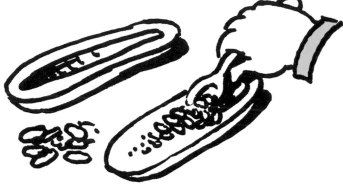

3 Place the cucumber halves on the cutting board. Using the utility knife, chop the cucumber by first cutting it lengthwise into several slices and then cutting across the slices, making the pieces as thin as possible. Place the cucumber pieces in a mixing bowl and sprinkle the salt over the pieces. Let stand for 20 minutes. Cucumbers are full of water and the salt helps to draw out a lot of that water.

4 Place the onion on the cutting board. Using the utility knife, carefully trim the ends off the onion and throw them away. Cut the onion lengthwise in half and peel the skin off one of the halves. Save the other half for the

pimiento spread or some other use. With the onion half on the cutting board, flat side down, cut it from end to end into thin slices, and then cut the slices crosswise as thinly as possible. Ask for help if you think you need it. Place the onion in the other mixing bowl.

5 Add the cream cheese to the onion and mix the two together with the back of the wooden spoon.

6 Place the strainer in the sink and put the cucumber pieces in it to drain. Press down on the cucumber with paper towels to dry the pieces more. Add the cucumber to the cream-cheese mixture and stir together with the wooden spoon.

7 Spoon the mixture into the small bowl, cover with plastic wrap, and refrigerate it until 30 minutes before you are ready to use it. Let it soften at room temperature. If the spread is very cold, stir it with the back of a spoon to soften it before spreading on the bread. The spread will keep for several weeks in the refrigerator.

Tip Sometimes an onion is so strong that, if it is used raw, it will overpower all the other ingredients in a dish. To remove the harsh taste, you can place the cut onion in cold water to cover, let it sit for 20 minutes, and then dry it. If the onion is going to be cooked, you don't need to soak it because cooking will reduce the harshness.

Did You Know?
The world's first known vegetable garden was created in Mesopotamia 4,000 years ago for growing cucumbers.

Pimiento Sandwich Filling

Ingredients

1 jar (3½ ounces) chopped pimientos

12 ounces sharp Cheddar cheese

½ small onion

1 cup mayonnaise

Makes: 1½ cups, enough for 6 sandwiches

Utensils

Strainer

Grater

Waxed paper

Mixing bowl

Cutting board

Utility knife

Measuring cups

Wooden spoon

Small bowl

Plastic wrap

Preparation time: 20 minutes

1 Place the strainer in the sink. Open the jar of pimientos and empty it into the strainer to drain.

2 Meanwhile, using the largest holes on the grater, carefully grate the cheese over a sheet of waxed paper. (Do this slowly, so you don't scrape your knuckles.) Place the cheese in the mixing bowl.

3 Place the onion half on the cutting board, peel off the skin, and throw away the skin. With the onion on the board, flat side down, cut it from end to end into thin slices and then cut across the slices 5 or 6 times to make small pieces. Add the onion to the cheese.

4 Add the mayonnaise to the cheese and onion and mix lightly with the wooden spoon. Add the pimientos and stir gently until well mixed. Spoon the mixture into the small bowl, cover it with plastic wrap, and place it in the refrigerator. Thirty minutes before you are ready to use it, take the pimiento filling out of the refrigerator and let it sit at room temperature. If the spread is very cold, it will be too hard to spread on the bread.

Tip Spread both this filling and the cucumber filling on crackers or toast halves for a great snack.

Polar Bear Pickles

Nothing tastes better with a sandwich than a crispy pickle. These are so good that you'll want to make more at holiday time and give them as gifts.

Ingredients

1 quart old-fashioned whole dill pickles

1 large onion

2 tablespoons cider vinegar

2 cups sugar

Makes: 1 quart

Utensils

Strainer

Cutting board

Utility knife

Plastic storage container approximately 8 x 10 inches, with a lid

Measuring spoons

Measuring cups

Wooden spoon

Preparation time: 20 minutes

Marinating time: Overnight

1 Place the strainer in the sink and empty the jar of pickles into it and let them drain.

2 Place one of the pickles on the cutting board. Using the utility knife, slice the pickle lengthwise into quarters. Cut spears lengthwise in half. Do the same with the remaining pickles.

3 Place the onion on the cutting board. Using the utility knife, carefully trim the ends off the onion and throw them away. Cut the onion crosswise in half and peel the skin from the halves and throw it away. Place each onion half flat side down on the cutting board and cut it into thin slices.

4 Place the pickle pieces in an even layer in the storage container and pour in the vinegar. Sprinkle the sugar over the pickles and then top with the onion slices. Cover the container and let it sit for 3 hours, which will give the sugar time to become liquid.

5 Stir the mixture, cover the container again, and refrigerate it overnight. By the next day, the pickles and onion should be crisp and sweet. They will last for weeks if covered and kept in the refrigerator.

Tip To make a very special gift of these pickles, place them in a clean jar, cover the jar, and then tie it with a ribbon.

Tuna-Melt Surprise

You might think there's nothing surprising about tuna, but the hidden crunch in this creamy combination comes from the layer of sprouts tucked between the cheese and the fish.

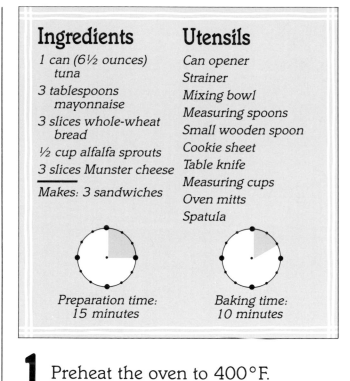

Ingredients

1 can (6½ ounces) tuna
3 tablespoons mayonnaise
3 slices whole-wheat bread
½ cup alfalfa sprouts
3 slices Munster cheese

Makes: 3 sandwiches

Preparation time: 15 minutes

Baking time: 10 minutes

Utensils

Can opener
Strainer
Mixing bowl
Measuring spoons
Small wooden spoon
Cookie sheet
Table knife
Measuring cups
Oven mitts
Spatula

1 Preheat the oven to 400°F.

2 Open the can of tuna with the can opener. Place the strainer in the sink and empty the can into the strainer

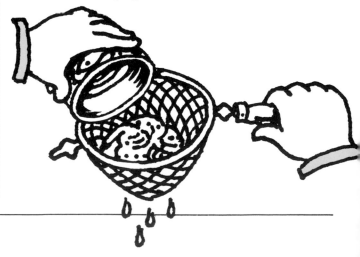

to let the tuna drain. If the tuna was packed in oil, rinse it very quickly under cold running water and let it drain.

3 Place the tuna in the mixing bowl and add the mayonnaise. Mix the tuna and mayonnaise together, breaking up the lumps of fish with the wooden spoon.

4 Place the slices of bread on the cookie sheet. Spread the tuna evenly over the bread. Sprinkle the sprouts over the tuna and then top each sandwich with a slice of the cheese, so that it covers the whole sandwich.

5 Put on the oven mitts and place the cookie sheet in the oven. Bake for 10 minutes and then look to see if the cheese is bubbly and has melted. If it hasn't, bake for another 2 minutes. When the sandwiches are ready, put the oven mitts on and place the cookie sheet on a heatproof surface. Lift each sandwich with the spatula and place it on a plate.

Stuffed Baked Potatoes

FULL-TIME ADULT • ASSISTANT NEEDED

When the weather turns cold, this perfect all-in-one meal helps take away the winter chills. Make sure you use baking potatoes, because they are big enough to hold lots of the wonderful filling.

Ingredients

4 medium-size baking potatoes

6 ounces Cheddar cheese (about 1½ cups grated)

1 large bunch broccoli

1 teaspoon salt

2 tablespoons butter

1 teaspoon mustard

Makes: 4 stuffed potatoes

Utensils

Vegetable brush
Paper towels
Fork
Baking sheet
Oven mitts
Grater
Waxed paper
Measuring cups
Paring knife (optional)
Medium-size saucepan with lid
Measuring spoons
Medium-size bowl
Slotted spoon
Strainer

Preparation time: 20 minutes

Baking time: 1 hour and 10 minutes

1 Preheat the oven to 400°F.

2 Scrub the potatoes with the vegetable brush under warm running water and pat dry with paper towels.

3 Using a fork, prick each potato 3 or 4 times and place them on the baking sheet. Put on the oven mitts and place the baking sheet in the oven. Bake for 1 hour.

4 While the potatoes are baking, make the filling. Using the largest holes on the grater, carefully grate the cheese over a sheet of waxed paper. (Do this slowly, so you don't scrape your knuckles.) You should have about 1½ cups.

5 Rinse the broccoli under cold running water and pat dry with paper towels. Remove the flowery heads from the broccoli stems either by breaking them off with your hands or by carefully cutting them off with the paring knife. Save the stems for another use.

6 Put the broccoli heads in the saucepan and place the pan on the stove. Pour enough water into the pan to just cover the broccoli. Add the salt and cover the pan. Heat to a boil over medium-high heat, then reduce the heat to low and simmer until the broccoli is tender when pierced with a fork, about 5 minutes.

7 Fill the bowl with cold water. Using the slotted spoon, move the broccoli to the cold water. Let it cool in the water for about 5 minutes.

8 Place the strainer in the sink and pour in the broccoli. Let it drain and then shake the strainer a couple of times to get rid of as much water as possible.

9 After the potatoes have baked for 1 hour, check to see if they are done. Put on the oven mitts and carefully pull the rack with the baking sheet on it out a little way. Poke the fork through the skin and into the heart of 1 potato. If the fork slides in easily, carefully remove the baking sheet from the oven and place it on a heatproof surface. Don't turn the oven off. If the potato is still firm, bake for another 20 minutes before testing again.

10 Leave the cooked potatoes on the baking sheet. Keep one oven mitt on and use that hand to pick up a potato. Rest the potato on a counter and with the fork in your uncovered hand, slit open the potato. Put the second mitt back on and squeeze the potato gently to open it more and to loosen the insides. Do this with each potato.

11 Take off the mitts and put a dab of butter and mustard in each potato. Spoon the broccoli into the potatoes and sprinkle them all with the cheese, trying not to drop any cheese on the baking sheet.

12 Put the oven mitts back on and place the baking sheet with the potatoes in the oven. Bake until the cheese is bubbly and has melted, about 10 minutes.

13 With the mitts on, place the baking sheet on a heatproof surface and place the potatoes on plates. Enjoy.

Tips You can prepare this dish faster by using frozen broccoli instead of fresh. Let the broccoli thaw completely at room temperature. Then all you have to do is pat it dry with paper towels and cut the stalks into small pieces.

The next time you make this dish, crumble some cooked bacon (page 66, steps 2 and 4) on top before you add the cheese—tastes great.

Did You Know?
The Incas of Peru once measured units of time by how long it took to cook a potato!

Cheese Soufflé in a Tomato

It's always so exciting to see these soufflés come out of the oven golden brown and puffed way up. Soufflés lose a lot of their fluffiness pretty quickly, but they taste just as great flat.

Ingredients

6 firm medium-size
  tomatoes
¼ teaspoon salt
6 ounces Swiss cheese
  (about 1½ cups
  grated)
12 mushrooms
3 scallions (green
  onions)
3 slices white bread
½ cup milk
2 eggs

Makes: 6 soufflés

Utensils

Cutting board
Utility knife
Teaspoon
Measuring spoons
Paper towels
Grater
Waxed paper
Measuring cups
Blender
2 mixing bowls
Electric mixer
Wooden spoon
Rubber spatula
Cookie sheet
Oven mitts
Large metal spoon

Preparation time:
30 minutes

Baking time:
30 minutes

1 Preheat the oven to 350°F.

2 Hold 1 of the tomatoes on its side on the cutting board. Using the utility knife, cut a ½-inch-thick slice off the top. Using the teaspoon, scoop the seeds and pulp out of the tomato and throw them away. Repeat with the remaining tomatoes. Sprinkle the insides of the tomato shells with the salt and place them upside down on several layers of paper towels to drain.

3 Using the largest holes on the grater, carefully grate the cheese over a sheet of waxed paper. (Do this slowly, so you don't scrape your knuckles.) You should have about 1½ cups.

4 Rinse the mushrooms and scallions quickly under cold running water and pat them dry with paper towels. Break the whole mushrooms into small pieces with your hands. Set them aside on a piece of waxed paper.

5 Place the scallions on the cutting board and, using the utility knife, trim off the roots. Cut the white bulbs and about 1 inch of the green stems into small slices. Add them to the mushrooms.

6 Place the slices of bread on the cutting board. Using the utility knife, trim off the crusts and save them to feed the birds or ducks. Tear the bread into small pieces and place them in the blender. Add the milk and place the cover on the machine. Turn the blender on and process until the mixture is thick. Add the grated cheese and process just until the cheese is mixed in.

7 Separate the eggs into the mixing bowls (page 7). Beat the egg yolks with the electric mixer at high speed until the yolks are smooth and creamy. Add the cheese mixture from the blender and the mushrooms and scallions and stir it all together with the wooden spoon.

8 Wash and dry the beaters; then beat the egg whites at high speed until they look like fluffy white clouds with peaks that don't fall when you stop beating.

9 Using the rubber spatula, scrape the egg whites into the bowl with the cheese mixture. Fold the two together with the spatula by bringing the cheese mixture up over the egg whites. Don't stir it too hard or the egg whites won't stay fluffy. Ask an adult for help if you think you need it.

10 Place the tomatoes cut side up on the cookie sheet and spoon the soufflé batter into them. Fill each to the top. Put the oven mitts on and place the cookie sheet in the oven. Bake for 30 minutes.

11 Check the soufflés to see if the tops are golden. If they are, the soufflés are ready. Put the oven mitts on and place the cookie sheet on a heatproof surface. Using the large spoon, scoop the tomatoes off the sheet and onto lunch plates. Serve them quickly before they flatten.

Tip The soufflé batter can also be baked in a small round baking dish with high sides. Butter the dish very well so that the soufflé can rise above the top.

Did You Know?
The French use the word soufflé *the same way we use the word* puffed.

Pita Pizza

FULL-TIME ADULT · ASSISTANT NEEDED

Middle Eastern pitas, or pocket breads, usually hold all kinds of sandwich fillings, but because they are shaped so conveniently round and flat, you can also give them an Italian twist and turn them into lunch-size pizzas.

Ingredients
4 large whole-wheat pita breads
2 ripe medium-size tomatoes
1 medium-size zucchini
4 ounces mozzarella cheese (about ⅔ cup grated)
Salt
Pepper
4 thin slices ham
¼ teaspoon dried oregano
¼ teaspoon dried basil

Makes: 4 pizzas

Preparation time: 25 minutes

Baking time: 15 minutes

Utensils
Scissors
Cookie sheet
Paper towels
Cutting board
Utility knife
Grater
Waxed paper
Measuring cups
Measuring spoons
Oven mitts

1 Preheat the oven to 425°F.

2 Using the scissors, cut a circle out of the top piece of each pita bread, leaving a ½-inch rim around the edge. Place the pita bottoms on the cookie sheet (save the pita circles for another use).

3 Rinse the tomatoes and zucchini under cold running water. Pat them dry with paper towels. Place the tomatoes on the cutting board and, using the utility knife, cut out the center core and throw it away. Slice each tomato crosswise. Then trim off the ends of the zucchini, throw them away, and cut the zucchini into thin round slices.

4 Using the largest holes on the grater, carefully grate the mozzarella over a sheet of waxed paper. (Do this slowly, so you don't scrape your knuckles.) You should have about ⅔ cup.

5 Arrange the tomato slices neatly in one layer on the pitas and sprinkle them lightly with salt and pepper. Place the ham slices on the tomatoes. If the slices are larger than the pita, you can tear the ham into smaller pieces and lay them over the tomatoes. Place the zucchini slices over the ham and then sprinkle with the oregano and basil. Top the pizzas with the grated cheese.

6 Put on the oven mitts and place the cookie sheet in the oven. Bake for 15 minutes. Then look to see if the cheese is bubbly and has melted. If it hasn't, bake up to 5 minutes longer. When the pizzas are ready, put on the oven mitts and remove the cookie sheet from the oven to a heatproof surface. Let the pizzas cool for 5 minutes before serving.

Tip You can make up your own pizza combinations of meat and vegetables. Your imagination makes you the master chef.

Did You Know?
The largest pizza ever made measured 80 feet 1 inch across and was cut into 60,318 slices.

Tacos

Tacos are such good eating that nobody cares if the taco shell crumbles after one bite and the filling drips onto the plate. Put plenty of napkins on the table for messy hands. Ask your adult assistant to help cook the meat—it can be tricky.

Ingredients

1 medium-size onion
1 pound ground beef
1 cup tomato purée
1 tablespoon ground cumin
2 teaspoons chili powder
¼ teaspoon garlic powder
4 ounces Cheddar cheese (about 1 cup grated)
4 lettuce leaves
8 taco shells
¼ cup sour cream
¼ to ½ cup taco sauce, medium hot

Makes: 8 tacos

Utensils

Cutting board
Utility knife
10-inch frying pan
Pot holder
Long-handled wooden spoon
Strainer
Medium-size bowl
Soupspoons
Measuring spoons
Grater
Waxed paper
Measuring cups

Preparation time: 15 minutes

Cooking time: 15 minutes

1 Place the onion on the cutting board. Using the utility knife, trim off the ends of the onion. Cut the onion in half from end to end and peel off the skin. Throw it away along with the ends. Place the onion halves flat side down on the cutting board, and cut each half lengthwise into several slices; then cut across the slices several times to make small pieces. Place the pieces in the frying pan.

2 Crumble the meat into the frying pan with your hands and place the pan on the stove. Stir the meat slightly with the wooden spoon to mix it with the onion. Cook over medium-high heat. When the meat starts to sizzle, stir it again. Brown the meat, stirring frequently, until all the pink is gone, 5 to 6 minutes. Ask an adult to stay nearby in case you need help.

3 Place the strainer over the bowl, and with the help of your assistant, spoon the meat and onion into the strainer to drain off the fat. Pour off any fat remaining in the pan.

4 Return the meat to the pan and add the tomato purée, cumin, chili powder, and garlic powder. Stir it all together and simmer over medium heat for 5 minutes, stirring occasionally. When the meat sauce is hot, turn the heat down to low.

5 Using the largest holes on the grater, carefully grate the cheese over a sheet of waxed paper. (Do this slowly, so you don't scrape your knuckles.) You should have about 1 cup.

6 Tear the lettuce leaves into small pieces with your hands.

7 To assemble the tacos, spoon the meat mixture into the taco shells, spoon some sour cream on the meat, sprinkle with the lettuce and then the cheese, and top with a spoonful of taco sauce. Or if you want, you can put all the ingredients in separate bowls on the table and let everyone assemble their own tacos.

Tip Tacos also taste good with chopped fresh tomato and avocado sprinkled on top.

Crustless Quiche

This quiche gets right to the heart of the matter—the filling. It's easy to make, and quick too. The cheese and half-and-half make it rich, so serve small slices along with Sports Car Fruit Salad (page 90) or just plain cut-up fruit.

Ingredients

1 teaspoon butter, at room temperature
4 eggs
¼ teaspoon mustard
2 cups half-and-half
4 ounces Cheddar cheese (about 1 cup grated)
3 mushrooms
2 scallions (green onions)

Serves: 6 to 8

Utensils

8-inch pie plate
Paper towels
Mixing bowl
Measuring spoons
Whisk
Measuring cups
Grater
Waxed paper
Cutting board
Utility knife
Cookie sheet
Oven mitts

Preparation time: 20 minutes

Baking time: 20 minutes

1 Preheat the oven to 325°F.

2 Spread the butter evenly on the bottom and side of the pie plate with a paper towel.

3 Break the eggs into the mixing bowl, add the mustard, and mix with the whisk until the eggs are blended. Add the half-and-half and whisk until well mixed.

4 Using the largest holes on the grater, carefully grate the cheese over a sheet of waxed paper. (Do this slowly, so you don't scrape your knuckles.) You should have about 1 cup.

5 Rinse the mushrooms and scallions under cold running water and then pat them dry with paper towels. Break the whole mushrooms into smaller pieces with your hands.

6 Place the scallions on the cutting board. Using the utility knife, trim off the roots and dark green tops and throw them away. Cut the scallions into small pieces.

7 Sprinkle the cheese in the bottom of the pie plate and then sprinkle the mushrooms and scallions over the cheese. Place the pie plate on the cookie sheet. Pour the egg mixture into the pie plate. With the help of an adult, place the cookie sheet in the oven. Bake for 20 minutes.

8 Put the oven mitts on and open the oven door. Shake the pie plate gently while you watch the center of the quiche. If the center moves like jelly, it needs to bake longer because the eggs haven't set enough to become firm. If the quiche isn't done, bake up to 7 minutes longer, depending on how liquidy the eggs were when you checked. When it is done, put on the oven mitts and ask an adult to help you place the cookie sheet on a heatproof surface. Let the quiche sit for about 10 minutes before you cut it into serving pieces.

Zucchini Pickles

FULL-TIME ADULT · ASSISTANT NEEDED

Most people think pickles are made only with cucumbers. Surprise your friends with these crispy sandwich mates.

Ingredients

1 pound zucchini
1 medium-size onion
3 cups water
2 tablespoons salt
1 cup sugar
1 tablespoon mustard seeds
½ teaspoon celery salt
½ teaspoon turmeric
1 ½ cups cider vinegar

Makes: 1 quart

Utensils

Paper towels
Cutting board
Utility knife
Mixing bowl
Measuring cups
Measuring spoons
Wooden spoon
Strainer
Saucepan
Pot holder
1-quart jar

Preparation time:
25 minutes

Marinating time:
4 hours

1 Rinse the zucchini under cold running water and pat dry with paper towels. Place the zucchini on the cutting board. Using the utility knife, trim off the ends of the zucchini and throw them away. Carefully slice the zucchini as thin as you can and put the slices in the mixing bowl.

2 Place the onion on the cutting board. Trim off the ends of the onion with the utility knife. Cut the onion in half from end to end and peel off the skin. Throw it away along with the ends. Place the onion halves flat side down on the cutting board and cut each half lengthwise into thin slices. Add the onion to the bowl.

3 Pour the water into the bowl. Add the salt and stir gently with the wooden spoon. Let stand for 2 hours.

4 Place the strainer in the sink and pour the zucchini and onion slices into it. Let drain and then return the slices to the mixing bowl.

5 Place the sugar, mustard seeds, celery salt, turmeric, and vinegar in the saucepan and stir to mix. Place the pan on the stove and heat to a boil over medium heat. Turn the heat off and ask your adult assistant to pour the boiling liquid over the zucchini and onion. Let stand for 2 hours.

6 Pour the zucchini, onion, and liquid back into the saucepan and place it on the stove. Heat to a boil over medium heat. Turn the heat off and spoon the pickles into the jar. Ask your assistant to pour enough of the hot liquid into the jar to fill it. Screw the lid on and refrigerate the pickles. They will keep for weeks.

Tip Pouring any hot liquid requires help from an adult assistant. Never try to carry a filled hot pot alone. The ingredients can splash out easily.

Potato Salad

FULL-TIME ADULT · ASSISTANT NEEDED

Potato salad always brings up good memories of warm weather and picnics. So even in winter when you can't get red-skinned or new potatoes, make it with winter potatoes and dream of summertime. If you mix in some pieces of ham and cheese too, you'll have a one-dish meal.

Ingredients

2 pounds red-skinned or new potatoes

5 cups water

1 rib celery

3 scallions (green onions)

1 cup mayonnaise

1 teaspoon mustard

2 tablespoons fresh dill leaves or 1 tablespoon dried dill weed

½ teaspoon salt

¼ teaspoon pepper

Makes: 8 servings

Preparation time: 45 minutes

Utensils

Large saucepan

Fork

Strainer

Pot holder

Large mixing bowl

Paper towels

Cutting board

Utility knife

Waxed paper

Measuring cups

Measuring spoons

Wooden spoon

Plastic wrap

Cooking time: 30 minutes

1 Rinse the potatoes under cold running water and place them in the saucepan. Place the saucepan on the stove and add the water. Cook the potatoes, uncovered, over medium heat until they can be pierced easily with a fork, about 30 minutes. Check the potatoes after 20 minutes so that they don't overcook and get mushy.

2 Place the strainer in the sink and ask an adult to pour the potatoes into the strainer. Run cool water over the potatoes for about 3 minutes. Place the potatoes in the mixing bowl and refrigerate, uncovered, for at least 30 minutes.

3 While the potatoes are cooling, rinse the celery and scallions under cold running water and pat dry with paper towels. Place the celery on the cutting board. Using the utility knife, trim off the leaf and stem ends and throw them away. Cut the celery lengthwise in half and then cut the strips crosswise to make small pieces. Set them aside on a piece of waxed paper.

4 Place the scallions on the cutting board. Trim the roots off and throw them away. Slice the scallions up to the dark green leaves. Add them to the celery. Throw the green tops away.

5 Take the potatoes out of the refrigerator. Place 1 potato on the cutting board and, using the utility knife, cut it in half. Turn the potato halves so that they are cut side down on the board and cut each half into quarters. Cut all the potatoes the same way and put all the pieces in the mixing bowl.

6 Add the celery, scallions, mayonnaise, mustard, dill, salt, and pepper to the potatoes and gently mix it all together with the wooden spoon.

7 Cover the bowl with plastic wrap and refrigerate it until you are ready to serve.

Tip If you do use winter potatoes for your salad, the skin isn't as tasty as red-skinned or new potatoes, so you should be sure to peel them before rinsing under cold water.

FULL-TIME ADULT · ASSISTANT NEEDED ·

Black Olive Bees and Carrot Curls

You can make this salad for lunch or dinner, but it is especially good with sandwiches. You can use a few of the curls and bees to decorate the sandwiches, too.

Ingredients

1 can (5¾ ounces) pitted jumbo black olives, about 20 olives

10 ice cubes

2 large carrots

Makes: About 20 olive bees

Preparation time: 25 minutes

Utensils

Can opener

Strainer

Medium-size mixing bowl

Vegetable peeler

Cutting board

Utility knife

1 Open the can of olives with the can opener. Place the strainer in the sink and empty the can into the strainer to let the olives drain.

2 Fill the mixing bowl halfway with cold water and drop in the ice cubes.

3 Use the peeler to peel the carrots. Place the carrots on the cutting board and, using the utility knife, cut off the ends and throw them away. Cut each carrot into 4-inch-long pieces. Using the peeler, peel long strips from the carrot pieces by holding the piece at one end and pushing the peeler away from you. Place all but 10 of the widest strips in the ice water. Refrigerate the bowl of carrots for 20 minutes while you make the olive bees.

4 Place the 10 wide carrot strips on the cutting board and, using the utility knife, cut the strips diagonally into triangles.

5 Place an olive on the cutting board. Using just the tip of the utility knife, cut 1 small slit in the middle of the olive; then turn the olive and cut another small slit on the opposite side. Press the ends together gently. The slits should open slightly. Push the tip of a carrot triangle into each slit. Place another triangle in the large opening at one end of the olive. Set the finished olive aside and make more olive bees.

6 Remove the bowl of carrot curls from the refrigerator and pour the carrots into the strainer in the sink. Place the carrot curls on a serving plate and decorate with the olive bees.

Tip The bees and curls can be made the day before you plan to serve them and kept in the refrigerator. Leave the carrot curls in the bowl of water, and put the olive bees on a plate and cover with plastic wrap. Then you only have to take them out of the refrigerator when you are ready to eat.

Crispy Cucumber Salad

Try to make this salad a couple of hours ahead of time. One hour for marinating the cucumbers is the minimum, but another hour or so will improve the flavor. If left too long, though, the cucumbers will get soggy.

Ingredients

2 medium-size cucumbers
1 teaspoon salt
½ teaspoon pepper
¼ teaspoon sugar
1 tablespoon cider vinegar
¼ teaspoon dried dill weed
1 tablespoon sour cream

Makes: 4 servings

Utensils

Vegetable peeler
Cutting board
Utility knife
Medium-size mixing bowl
Measuring spoons
Wooden spoon
Strainer

Preparation time:
15 minutes

Marinating time:
1 hour

1 Using the peeler, peel the green skin from the cucumbers and throw it away. Place the cucumbers on the cutting board. Using the utility knife, trim off the ends of each cucumber and throw them away. Cut each cucumber into thin round slices. Put the cucumber slices in the mixing bowl.

2 Add the salt, pepper, sugar, and vinegar to the cucumbers and toss to mix with the wooden spoon. Refrigerate for at least 1 hour.

3 Place the strainer in the sink and pour the cucumbers into it to drain. Return the cucumbers to the bowl. Add the dill and sour cream and stir gently until mixed.

Bread and Butter Pudding

If the sandwich fillings are gone before the bread is finished, here is an easy way to turn the last of the loaf into a sweet treat. The bread floats on top, making a toasty lid over the custard filling.

Ingredients

5 slices white bread

3 tablespoons butter, at room temperature

4 cups milk

7 eggs

¾ cup sugar

½ teaspoon vanilla extract

Makes: 6 servings

Utensils

Cutting board

Utility knife

Table knife

Measuring cups

Medium-size saucepan

Large mixing bowl

Measuring spoons

Whisk

8-inch square baking pan or 2-quart baking dish

Cookie sheet

Oven mitts

Preparation time: 20 minutes

Baking time: 30 minutes

1 Preheat the oven to 375°F.

2 Place the bread slices on the cutting board. Using the utility knife, trim the crusts off each slice. Save the crusts to feed the birds or ducks. Spread one side of each piece of bread with butter then cut the bread slices in half.

3 Pour the milk into the saucepan and heat it over medium heat until the milk steams and you can see tiny bubbles around the side of the pan. Turn the heat off.

4 Break the eggs into the mixing bowl. Add the sugar and vanilla and mix with the whisk until thoroughly blended.

5 Pour the warm milk into the egg mixture and whisk again until blended.

6 Place the baking pan on the cookie sheet and pour the egg mixture into the pan. Float the bread slices, buttered sides up, on top of the egg mixture.

7 With the help of your adult assistant, place the cookie sheet on a rack in the center of the oven. Bake for 30 minutes. Put the oven mitts on, pull the pudding out slightly, and insert the knife into the center of it. If the knife looks clean when you take it out, the pudding is done. If the pudding isn't ready, bake it for another 10 minutes. Ask your assistant to help you remove the cookie sheet from the oven and place it on a heatproof surface. Let the pudding cool for 15 minutes before serving.

SNACKS

Vegetable Kabobs with Chunky Herb Dip

It's fun to eat your lunchtime salad off a stick, but if you don't have any skewers, make vegetable mountains instead. Heap piles of each on a large serving plate with the dip in the middle. This is great finger food—just take a piece and dip away.

Ingredients

1 head broccoli
⅓ head cauliflower
12 mushrooms
1 pint cherry tomatoes
1 medium-size zucchini
1 medium-size green bell pepper
1 medium-size red bell pepper
2 scallions (green onions)
½ cup sour cream
½ cup cottage cheese
½ teaspoon dried basil
½ teaspoon dried mint
⅛ teaspoon salt

Makes: 6 kabobs

Preparation time: 25 minutes

Utensils

Paper towels
Utility knife
Cutting board
6 wooden skewers
Blender or food processor
Measuring cups
Measuring spoons
Rubber spatula
Medium-size bowl

1 Rinse all the vegetables under cold running water and pat dry with paper towels.

2 Remove the flowery heads from the broccoli stalks by breaking them off with your hands or carefully cutting them with the utility knife. Save the stems for another use. Do the same thing with the cauliflower.

3 Pull the stems off the mushrooms and save them for another use. Pull any green stems and leaves from the tomatoes and set 6 tomatoes aside for the dip.

4 Trim off the ends of the zucchini and throw them away. Cut the zucchini into thick slices. Carefully cut each pepper in half. Break off the stems and rinse out the seeds. Dry the peppers on paper towels, then cut them into big squares and set 3 squares aside for the dip.

5 Carefully push the vegetables, except the scallions and the 6 tomatoes, onto the skewers in any order that looks good to you.

6 Trim the roots and dark green leaves from the scallions. Cut each scallion into 3 or 4 pieces. Carefully cut the 6 tomatoes in half. Place the scallions, tomato halves, and 3 pepper squares in the blender or food processor. Cover the machine and process until the vegetables are small chunks. Add the sour cream, cottage cheese, basil, mint, and salt to the blender. Replace the top and process until the dip is well blended, about 10 seconds. Using the rubber spatula, scrape all the dip into the bowl.

7 Place the kabobs on a serving plate and serve with the chunky dip. You can spoon the dip over the kabobs or let everyone dip their own.

Tips Use any of the vegetables in your refrigerator to make your own combinations for kabobs.

You can make a great soup with the leftover vegetables: Cut the vegetable stalks and stems into small pieces. Pour 1 can (12 ounces) beef broth into a medium saucepan and heat it to a boil over medium heat. Add the vegetables and turn the heat down to low. Simmer for 5 minutes. Turn off the heat and stir in 1 teaspoon of teriyaki sauce. This is really delicious!

Baked Cheese Fingers with Bacon and Tomato

You can't go wrong at snack time with Baked Cheese Fingers. If bacon and tomato aren't available, substitute ham and slices of a favorite vegetable like zucchini or avocado. Melted cheese seems to go with almost everything.

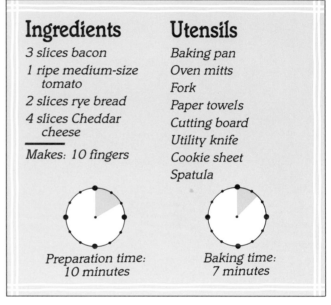

Ingredients

3 slices bacon
1 ripe medium-size tomato
2 slices rye bread
4 slices Cheddar cheese

Makes: 10 fingers

Utensils

Baking pan
Oven mitts
Fork
Paper towels
Cutting board
Utility knife
Cookie sheet
Spatula

Preparation time: 10 minutes

Baking time: 7 minutes

1 Preheat the oven to 400°F.

2 Place the bacon slices in the baking pan. Put on the oven mitts and place the pan in the oven. Bake for 7 minutes or until crispy. Put the oven mitts on again and carefully place the pan on a heatproof surface. Keep the oven on. When the bacon has cooled, lift the slices out of the pan with a fork and place them on a folded paper towel to drain.

3 Rinse the tomato, pat it dry with a paper towel, and place it on the cutting board. Using the utility knife, cut out the core, then slice the tomato.

4 Crumble the cooled bacon.

5 Place the bread slices on the cookie sheet and layer the tomato slices on top. Sprinkle the bacon over the tomato and layer the cheese over the bacon.

6 Put the oven mitts on and place the cookie sheet in the oven. Bake for 7 minutes. Look to see if the cheese is bubbly and has melted. If it hasn't, bake for another 3 minutes. When it is ready, put the oven mitts on and place the cookie sheet on a heatproof surface. Let cool about 5 minutes.

7 Slide the spatula under each slice of bread and put them on the cutting board. Using the utility knife, cut each sandwich into 5 strips and serve.

Banana Nut Bread

Banana bread smells so good when it's baking that it's hard to be patient long enough for the bread to cool down. When it's ready, smear a slice with cream cheese and sprinkle raisins on top. The wait will seem more than worthwhile.

Ingredients

½ cup (1 stick) plus 1 tablespoon butter, at room temperature

2 cups all-purpose flour

¾ teaspoon baking soda

½ teaspoon salt

¾ cup sugar

2 eggs

3 very ripe bananas

2 tablespoons sour cream

1 cup chopped walnuts

Cream cheese for serving (optional)

Raisins for serving (optional)

Makes: 1 loaf

Utensils

Paper towel

Measuring spoons

Loaf pan (8½ x 4½ inches)

Measuring cups

Small mixing bowl

Wooden spoon

Large mixing bowl

Electric mixer

Table knife (optional)

Rubber spatula

Oven mitts

Cooling rack

Preparation time: 20 minutes

Baking time: 1 hour and 10 minutes

1 Preheat the oven to 350°F.

2 Using the paper towel, rub 1 tablespoon butter evenly on the bottom and sides of the loaf pan.

3 Mix the flour, baking soda, and salt in the small mixing bowl with the wooden spoon.

4 Place ½ cup butter and the sugar in the large mixing bowl and beat with the electric mixer until it is pale yellow and creamy.

5 Break the eggs into the large bowl and beat until the eggs are completely blended with the butter mixture.

6 Add the flour mixture and beat until smooth.

7 Peel the bananas and, with your hands or with the table knife, break the bananas into large chunks. Add the bananas and sour cream to the batter and mix until smooth. Add the walnuts and mix at the lowest speed until they are scattered evenly through the batter.

8 Pour the batter into the buttered pan and scrape out the bowl with the rubber spatula. Smooth the top of the batter with the spatula.

9 Put the oven mitts on and place the pan in the oven. Bake for 1 hour and 10 minutes. Then look to see if the bread has shrunk away from the sides of the pan. If it hasn't, bake for another 10 minutes.

10 When the bread is ready, put the oven mitts on and place the pan on the cooling rack. Let it cool for 15 minutes. Then, with the oven mitts on, turn the pan upside down, letting the bread fall out. Set the bread right side up and let it cool for another 15 minutes before slicing. Serve with cream cheese and a bowl of raisins.

Did You Know?
Bananas are the oldest fruit known to have been traded, dating back tens of thousands of years.

Nachos

A Mexican-style snack that's popular throughout the United States, nachos are traditionally prepared using tostadas—crisp tortillas cut into wedges—hot chile pepper, Monterey Jack cheese, and sometimes refried beans. This recipe is quick and easy to make and perfect for days when friends are visiting and you'd like snack time to be more special.

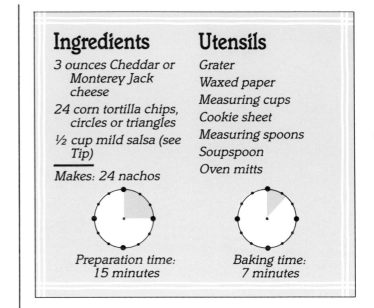

Ingredients
3 ounces Cheddar or Monterey Jack cheese

24 corn tortilla chips, circles or triangles

½ cup mild salsa (see Tip)

Makes: 24 nachos

Preparation time: 15 minutes

Utensils
Grater
Waxed paper
Measuring cups
Cookie sheet
Measuring spoons
Soupspoon
Oven mitts

Baking time: 7 minutes

1 Preheat the oven to 425°F.

2 Using the largest holes on the grater, carefully grate the cheese over a sheet of waxed paper. (Do this slowly, so you don't scrape your knuckles.) You should have about ¾ cup.

3 Place the chips flat on the cookie sheet. Using the measuring spoon, spread ½ teaspoon salsa on each chip. Then sprinkle the cheese evenly over the chips with the tablespoon, trying not to drop any cheese on the cookie sheet.

Tip Salsa—the Spanish word for sauce—is also used to mean chile sauce and is easy to find in all degrees of "hotness" in most supermarkets. Mild salsa adds just the right amount of pizazz to these nachos.

4 Put the oven mitts on and place the cookie sheet in the oven. Bake for 7 minutes. Then look to see if the cheese is bubbly and has melted. If it hasn't, bake for another 3 minutes. When the nachos are ready, put the oven mitts on and place the cookie sheet on a heat-proof surface. Let the nachos cool for 2 minutes and then put them on a serving plate.

Apple Spritzer

Make spritzers with any fruit juice and top the drink with any sliced fresh fruit that you like. Apple spritzers are particularly tasty when drunk through a straw.

Ingredients
1 small apple
12 large ice cubes
4 cups apple juice
2 cups club soda or seltzer water

Makes: 4 drinks

Preparation time:
10 minutes

Utensils
Paper towels
Cutting board
Apple corer
Utility knife
Measuring cups

1 Rinse off the apple and pat it dry with a paper towel. Place the apple on the cutting board. Push the corer through the center of the apple, twist the core out of the apple, and discard. Using the utility knife, cut the apple in half. Place the apple halves flat side down on the cutting board and cut each one in half from end to end.

2 Put 3 ice cubes in each of 4 tall glasses. Measure and pour 1 cup apple juice and then ½ cup soda water into each glass. Add 1 apple quarter to each drink and serve right away.

Mulled Apple Cider

This is a perfect drink to have on cold afternoons when it seems that nothing will warm you up. Mulled cider also makes a festive holiday drink to serve on Thanksgiving or Christmas.

Ingredients

1 orange
1½ quarts apple cider
2 cinnamon sticks
⅛ teaspoon ground nutmeg
⅛ teaspoon ground mace
1 whole clove

Makes: 4 servings

Preparation time:
10 minutes

Utensils

Cutting board
Utility knife
Medium saucepan
Pot holder
Plastic wrap
Measuring spoons
Wooden spoon
Ladle

Cooking time:
25 minutes

1 Place the orange on the cutting board and, using the utility knife, cut it in half. Put one of the orange halves in the saucepan and wrap the other half in plastic wrap and save it to eat later.

2 Put the saucepan on the stove and carefully pour in the apple cider. Add the cinnamon sticks, nutmeg, mace, and whole clove and stir with the wooden spoon.

3 Heat the cider over medium heat until it steams and begins to bubble, about 10 minutes. Then reduce the heat to medium-low. Simmer the cider for at least 15 minutes. You can keep it warm over low heat for several hours. Ladle the cider into 4 mugs and serve warm.

Pineapple Zinger

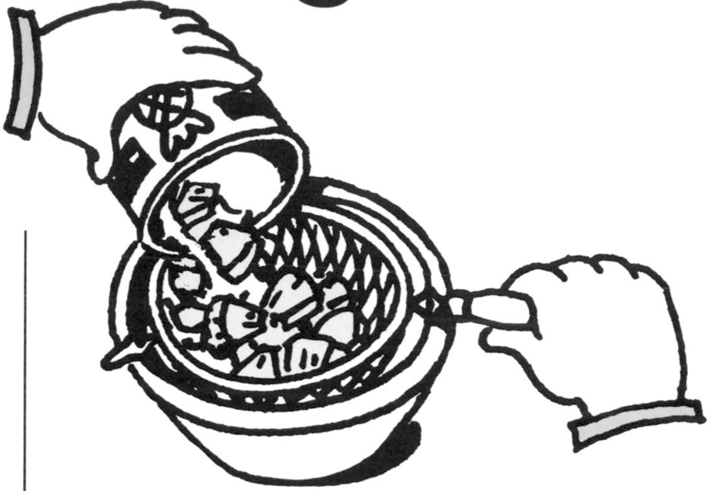

A refreshing fruit drink that adds snap to a sluggish morning, Pineapple Zingers also taste good after you've been playing hard on a hot summer afternoon.

Ingredients

2 cans (16 ounces each) unsweetened pineapple chunks

Ice cubes

1 quart seltzer water or club soda

Makes: 4 drinks

Utensils:

Can opener
Strainer
Large mixing bowl
Large spoon
Blender
Measuring cups
Long-handled wooden spoon
Iced tea spoon

Preparation time: 15 minutes

1 Carefully open the cans of pineapple using the can opener. Set the strainer in the mixing bowl and pour the pineapple into the strainer. Let it drain but save the syrup. Spoon the fruit into the blender and then measure 1 cup of the strained syrup and pour that into the blender. Place the lid on the blender and turn it on to high speed. Blend for 1 minute. Turn off the blender, remove the lid and, using the long-handled spoon, stir the fruit around so that it can all purée evenly. Replace the lid on the blender and turn it back on high for 30 seconds or until the fruit is well puréed.

2 Fill 4 tall glasses with ice cubes, and then fill each one three-quarters full with the pineapple purée. Pour in enough seltzer water to fill the glass. Mix the drink carefully, using the iced tea spoon. Now your zinger is ready to serve.

Tip Always make sure the top is in place before turning on the blender. Otherwise, whatever food is inside will splatter on you. It is also important to remember never to stir anything while the blender is in operation. Wait until you have turned it off and the blade has stopped rotating before using a wooden spoon or rubber scraper for any necessary mixing.

Dreamy Hot Chocolate

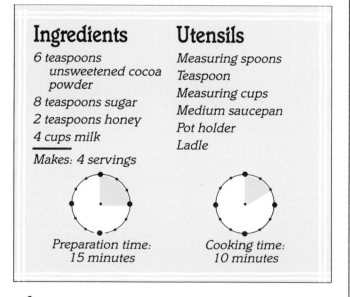

Hot chocolate tastes especially good with a sprinkling of cinnamon on top. Give it a try.

Ingredients
6 teaspoons unsweetened cocoa powder
8 teaspoons sugar
2 teaspoons honey
4 cups milk

Makes: 4 servings

Utensils
Measuring spoons
Teaspoon
Measuring cups
Medium saucepan
Pot holder
Ladle

Preparation time: 15 minutes

Cooking time: 10 minutes

1 Measure 1½ teaspoons cocoa powder, 2 teaspoons sugar, and ½ teaspoon honey into each of 4 mugs. Stir with the teaspoon to make a paste. Add 1 tablespoon milk to each mug and stir until it is blended.

2 Pour the remaining milk into the saucepan and heat over medium heat until the milk begins to steam and you can see tiny bubbles at the side of the pan. Turn the heat off.

3 Carefully ladle the milk into the mugs and stir with the teaspoon. Serve right away.

Tip Hot chocolate has long been a winter favorite, but it doesn't have to disappear during the summer. Simply add ice cubes and serve it in tall glasses for a refreshing pick-me-up on a hot, hot day.

DINNER

78

Split Pea Soup

FULL-TIME ADULT · ASSISTANT NEEDED

The next time your mom or dad bakes a ham, ask them to save the bone so you can make them a hearty Split Pea Soup. When accompanied by the Baked Cheese Fingers with Bacon and Tomato (page 66) or the Copper Penny Salad (page 92), this soup becomes a filling meal.

Ingredients

2 cups green split peas
7 cups water
3 cups beef broth (see Tip)
1 ham bone
1 rib celery
1 medium-size onion
¾ cup croutons

Makes: 6 servings

Utensils

Measuring cups
Strainer
6-quart saucepan
Pot holder
Wooden spoon
Cutting board
Utility knife
Slotted spoon
Ladle

Preparation time: 20 minutes

Cooking time: 1 hour and 45 minutes

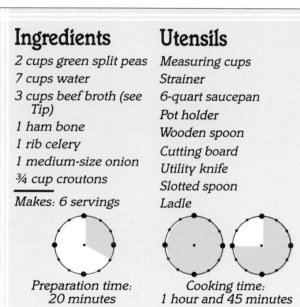

1 Put the split peas into the strainer and rinse them under cold running water. Stir them around with your hand and rinse again.

2 Put the saucepan on the stove, but don't turn on the burner yet.

3 Place the drained split peas in the saucepan. Carefully add the water and beef broth and stir with the wooden spoon. Add the ham bone.

4 Rinse the celery under cold running water, break it into large pieces, and add it to the pan.

5 Place the onion on the cutting board and trim off the ends with the utility knife. Peel off the outer skin and throw it away along with the ends. Add the onion to the pan.

6 Heat the soup to a boil over medium heat. Then reduce the heat to medium-low and let it simmer uncovered for 1½ hours. Stir it occasionally with the long-handled spoon.

7 Remove the onion and celery pieces with the slotted spoon and throw them away. Remove the ham bone and let it cool. Keep the soup simmering on the stove. When the ham bone is cool enough to touch, pull off any meat that is clinging to the bone and return the meat to the soup.

8 Ladle the soup into bowls and scatter a few croutons over the soup in each bowl.

Tip For the beef broth you can use either canned broth or 3 beef bouillon cubes or 3 packets beef bouillon powder diluted in 3 cups of boiling water.

Baked Manicotti

FULL-TIME ADULT · ASSISTANT NEEDED

These Italian pasta are fun to fill, and when they are cooked, ooze creamy ricotta and sausage stuffing. Manicotti is a great family get-together dish.

Ingredients

6 ounces pork sausage meat (or link sausages)

15-ounce container ricotta cheese

1 teaspoon dried mint

½ teaspoon dried oregano

6 ounces mozzarella cheese (about 1½ cups, grated)

14 manicotti shells

10 mushrooms

1 jar (16 ounces) spaghetti sauce

¼ cup water

Makes: 6 servings

Utensils

8-inch frying pan

Long-handled wooden spoon

Slotted spoon

Mixing bowl

Measuring spoons

Grater

Waxed paper

Measuring cups

Teaspoon

13 x 9-inch baking pan

Paper towels

Aluminum foil

Oven mitts

Preparation time: 30 minutes

Baking time: 1 hour and 15 minutes

1 With your hands, crumble the sausage meat into the frying pan. If you are using link sausages, squeeze the meat out of its skin, throw away the skin, and crumble the meat. Place the pan on the stove. Cook the sausage over medium-high heat, stirring with the long-handled spoon, until all the meat is browned, 4 to 5 minutes.

2 Using the slotted spoon, transfer the cooked sausage to the mixing bowl, leaving the fat in the pan. Add the ricotta, mint, and oregano to the bowl and stir it all together.

3 Using the largest holes on the grater, carefully grate the mozzarella over a sheet of waxed paper. (Do this slowly so you don't scrape your knuckles.) You should have about 1½ cups. Add ¾ cup of the mozzarella to the ricotta mixture and stir to mix.

4 Preheat the oven to 350°F.

5 Using the teaspoon, spoon the ricotta filling into the manicotti shells. Place the shells in the baking pan.

6 Rinse the mushrooms and pat dry with paper towels. Break the whole mushrooms into pieces and sprinkle them over the manicotti shells. Gently pour the spaghetti sauce over the shells and then sprinkle the remaining mozzarella over the sauce.

7 Pour the water all around the side of the pan. Cover the pan with aluminum foil and seal the edges by folding the foil tightly around the rim.

8 Put the oven mitts on and place the pan on a rack in the center of the oven. Bake for 1 hour and 15 minutes. Put the oven mitts on again, and place the baking pan on a heatproof surface. Carefully remove the aluminum foil, opening the edge that is farthest away from you first to let the trapped steam escape. Serve the manicotti hot.

Chili

FULL-TIME ADULT ASSISTANT NEEDED

You may think chili is a Mexican dish but it really originated in Texas, U.S.A. Our variation includes beans mixed in with the meat, although Texans prefer their chili over rice with the spicy beans on the side.

Ingredients

1 medium green bell pepper
1 small onion
1 pound lean ground beef
1 can (14½ ounces) crushed tomatoes
1 can (19 ounces) kidney beans
2 tablespoons chili powder
1 tablespoon ground cumin
½ teaspoon garlic powder
1 cup tomato purée
½ teaspoon salt
4 ounces Cheddar cheese (about 1 cup, grated)
1 container (8 ounces) sour cream

Makes: 6 servings

Utensils

Paper towels
Cutting board
Utility knife
Large saucepan
Pot holder
Long-handled wooden spoon
Can opener
Strainer
Measuring spoons
Measuring cups
Grater
Waxed paper

Preparation time: 20 minutes

Cooking time: 30 minutes

1 Rinse the green pepper under cold water, pat it dry with paper towels, and place it on the cutting board. Using the utility knife, cut the pepper lengthwise in half. Break off the stem and rinse the seeds out. Dry the pepper halves with paper towels and place them on the cutting board. Cut each half lengthwise into several slices. Then cut across the slices to make small pieces. Place the pepper pieces in the saucepan.

2 Place the onion on the cutting board. Using the utility knife, trim off the ends and then cut it lengthwise in half. Peel off the skin, and throw it away along with the ends. Place the onion halves flat side down on the cutting board, and cut each half into several slices. Then cut across the slices to make small pieces. Place the onion pieces in the saucepan.

3 Crumble the ground meat into the pan with your hands and place the pan on the stove. Cook over medium heat, stirring occasionally with the long-handled spoon, until all the meat is browned, about 10 minutes.

4 Using the can opener, open the can of crushed tomatoes and empty the can into the saucepan.

5 Place the strainer in the sink. Open the can of kidney beans and empty the can into the strainer to let the beans drain.

6 Add the kidney beans, chili powder, cumin, garlic powder, tomato purée, and salt to the meat. Stir it all together and simmer over low heat for 20 minutes.

7 While the chili is cooking, use the largest holes on the grater to carefully grate the cheese over a sheet of waxed paper. (Do this slowly so you don't scrape your knuckles.) You should have about 1 cup.

8 When the chili is ready, ladle it into soup bowls; spoon some sour cream on top and sprinkle the cheese over each serving.

Rosemary Chicken

This version of roast chicken can easily become a family favorite. The cherry tomatoes stay whole even after cooking and each bite bursts with flavorful juice.

Ingredients

1 chicken (3½ to 4 pounds), bag of giblets removed

½ teaspoon salt

¼ teaspoon pepper

1 tablespoon dried rosemary

4 tablespoons (½ stick) butter, cold

12 cherry tomatoes

Makes: 4 servings

Preparation time: 15 minutes

Baking time: 1 hour and 10 minutes

Utensils

Paper towels

Measuring spoons

Roasting pan

Oven mitts

Serving bowl

Carving knife

Carving fork

1 Preheat the oven to 400°F.

2 Rinse the chicken inside and out under cold running water and pat dry, also inside and out, with paper towels. Ask your adult assistant to help you remove any extra fat from the chicken.

3 Sprinkle the salt and pepper into the cavity. Crumble the rosemary in your hand and sprinkle it into the cavity. Break the butter into pieces and put them in the cavity, too. Then rinse the cherry tomatoes under cold running water, pat them dry, and put them all in the cavity.

4 Place the chicken in the roasting pan. Put on the oven mitts and place the pan on a rack in the center of the oven. Bake for 1 hour and 10 minutes.

5 Put the oven mitts on and, with an adult's help, place the roasting pan on a heatproof surface. Let the chicken sit for 15 minutes, then carefully scoop out the tomatoes and place them in a

serving bowl. Place the chicken on a serving platter and surround it with some of the tomatoes.

Tip You might find it easier to bring the chicken to the table already cut up into serving pieces. Ask an adult to do the job for you, then place the chicken pieces on a platter. Serve the tomatoes and pan juices in a serving bowl.

Chicken and Biscuit Pie

FULL-TIME ADULT · ASSISTANT NEEDED

A mountainous casserole with plenty of sauce and vegetables streaming between the flaky biscuits, this one-dish meal is satisfying for even the heartiest dinner appetites.

Ingredients

1 chicken (3½ to 4 pounds), cut into 8 serving pieces

4 cups chicken broth (see Tip)

2 cups water

2 cans (10½ ounces each) cream of chicken soup

1 box (10 ounces) frozen peas and onions

2 tablespoons chopped fresh dill leaves or 1 tablespoon dried dill

2 tubes prepared biscuit dough

Makes: 4 to 6 servings

Utensils

6-quart saucepan

Measuring cups

Long-handled wooden spoon

Can opener

Medium-size saucepan

Pot holder

Slotted spoon

10-inch round baking dish, 2½ inches deep

Measuring spoons

Cookie sheet

Oven mitts

Preparation time: 35 minutes

Baking time: 50 minutes

1 Rinse the chicken pieces under cold running water. Ask your adult assistant to help you remove any extra fat from the chicken.

2 Place the large saucepan on the stove and carefully pour in the chicken broth and water. Heat to a boil over medium heat. Then add the chicken and cook over medium heat for 15 minutes; stir the chicken pieces with the long-handled spoon occasionally so that the pieces cook evenly.

3 While the chicken is cooking, open the cans of soup with the can opener and empty the cans into the medium saucepan. Add the frozen peas and onions to the soup and stir it all together. Bring the mixture to a boil over medium heat. Lower the heat and continue cooking for 10 minutes.

4 Using the slotted spoon, transfer the chicken to the baking dish. Ask an adult to help you measure 1½ cups of the chicken cooking liquid and pour it into the soup. Add the dill and stir the soup mixture. Save the remaining cooking liquid for another use.

5 Preheat the oven to 325°F.

6 Pour the soup mixture over the chicken pieces in the baking pan. Crack open the tubes of biscuit dough and arrange the biscuits over the chicken.

7 Place the baking pan on the cookie sheet. Put the oven mitts on and place the cookie sheet in the oven. Bake for 40 to 50 minutes.

8 Check to see if the biscuits are golden brown. If they are not, bake for another 10 minutes. When the biscuits are browned, put the oven mitts on and, with the help of an adult, place the cookie sheet on a heatproof surface. Serve the pie hot.

Tip For the chicken broth you can use either canned broth or 4 chicken bouillon cubes or 4 packets of chicken bouillon powder diluted in 4 cups of boiling water.

My Very Own Meat Loaf

Everyone loves meat loaf, an all-time favorite, and now you can serve your friends their own individual loaves. Actually, because these have an unusual shape, maybe they should be called meat cupcakes or meat muffins instead!

Ingredients
2 tablespoons butter, at room temperature
1 medium-size onion
1½ pounds lean ground beef
¼ cup dry bread crumbs
½ teaspoon garlic powder
½ teaspoon salt
¼ teaspoon pepper
1 large egg
6 tablespoons ketchup
3 slices bacon, cut in half

Makes: 6 individual meat loaves

Preparation time: 15 minutes

Baking time: 25 minutes

Utensils
6-cup muffin tin
Paper towels
Cutting board
Utility knife
Large mixing bowl
Measuring cups
Measuring spoons
Cookie sheet
Oven mitts
Soupspoon

1 Preheat the oven to 350°F.

2 Lightly butter 6 of the muffin cups, using a paper towel to spread the butter.

3 Place the onion on the cutting board. Using the utility knife, trim off the ends and then cut the onion in half from end to end. Peel off the skin and throw it away along with the ends. Place the onion halves flat side down on the cutting board and cut lengthwise into several slices. Then cut across the slices to make small pieces. Put the onion pieces in the mixing bowl.

4 Crumble the meat with your hands into the bowl. Add the bread crumbs, garlic powder, salt, and pepper. Break the egg into the bowl. Mix it all together with your hands and then wash your hands.

5 Spoon 1 tablespoon ketchup into each of the 6 buttered muffin cups.

6 Using your hands, divide the meat mixture evenly among the 6 cups, and then wash your hands again.

7 Place the bacon on the cutting board and cut each slice in half. Place 1 piece of bacon on each small meat loaf.

8 Place the muffin tin on the cookie sheet. Put the oven mitts on and place the cookie sheet in the oven. Bake for 25 minutes.

9 Put the oven mitts on and, with the help of an adult, place the cookie sheet on a heatproof surface. To serve, scoop the loaves out with the soup-spoon and place them, bacon side down, on a serving plate.

Sports Car Fruit Salad

Make plenty of this fruit salad because it has a way of really taking off—vroom!

Ingredients

1 cantaloupe
1 small bunch seedless
  grapes
8 strawberries
1 banana
½ cup orange juice
¼ cup shredded
  coconut

Makes: 4 servings

Preparation time:
20 minutes

Utensils

Cutting board
Utility knife
Soupspoon
Melon baller
Mixing bowl
1½-inch metal cookie
  cutter
6 toothpicks
Paper towels
Measuring cups
Wooden spoon

1 Place the cantaloupe on the cutting board. Using the utility knife, cut a 2-inch-thick slice from the top of the melon; then cut a ½-inch-thick slice from the bottom so that the melon can stand without falling over. Scrape the seeds out of the melon with the soupspoon. Using the melon baller, scoop out small melon balls and place them in the mixing bowl. Don't cut through the bottom of the melon shell—it will be the container for the salad.

2 Using the cookie cutter, cut 4 circles from the thick slice of melon. Attach the circles to the bottom of the melon shell with the toothpicks so that they look like wheels.

3 Rinse the grapes, pick them off the stem, and add all but 2 of them to the mixing bowl. Attach the 2 grapes to the front of the melon shell to look like headlights.

4 Rinse the strawberries and pull off any green leaves. Pat the berries dry on paper towels and add them to the melon balls and grapes.

5 Peel the banana, place it on the cutting board, and cut it into slices. Add the banana to the mixing bowl.

6 Add the orange juice and coconut and toss to mix with the wooden spoon. Spoon the fruit salad into the melon shell and serve right away.

FULL-TIME ADULT · ASSISTANT NEEDED

Copper Penny Salad

This salad has its roots in Texas, but its popularity has spread throughout the United States. The dressing for these copper pennies gives them a nice refreshing taste.

Ingredients

6 carrots
4 cups water
1 teaspoon salt
¼ cup cider vinegar
½ cup vegetable oil
2 teaspoons chopped fresh parsley leaves
2 teaspoons fresh dill leaves
¼ teaspoon sugar
⅛ teaspoon black pepper

Makes: 4 servings

Utensils

Vegetable peeler
Cutting board
Utility knife
Medium-size saucepan
Measuring cups
Measuring spoons
Pot holder
Strainer
Paper towels
Mixing bowl
Wooden spoon
Plastic wrap

Preparation time: 40 minutes

Cooking time: 15 minutes

1 Using the peeler, peel the carrots. Place the carrots on the cutting board. Using the utility knife, cut the root and leaf ends off the carrots, throw the ends away, and then cut the carrots into thin slices.

2 Place the saucepan on the stove and carefully pour in the water. Add ½ teaspoon of the salt. Heat to a boil over medium heat. Add the carrots and cook just until tender, about 10 minutes.

3 Place the strainer in the sink. Ask your adult assistant to pour the carrots into the strainer. Cool them under cold running water and let them drain. Pat the carrots dry with paper towels.

4 Place the carrots in the mixing bowl. Add the vinegar, oil, remaining ½ teaspoon salt, the parsley, dill, sugar, and pepper to the carrots and toss with the wooden spoon to mix.

5 Cover the bowl with plastic wrap and refrigerate for 30 minutes before serving.

Acorn Squash

Squash is one of the treats to look forward to in the fall when the leaves are changing colors. After baking, the honey and butter remain puddled in the heart of each squash half, so you can scoop some out with every bite.

Ingredients

2 small acorn squash
4 tablespoons (½ stick) butter
4 tablespoons honey

Makes: 4 servings

Utensils

Cutting board
Large heavy knife
Soupspoon
Baking pan
Measuring spoons
Aluminum foil
Oven mitts
Fork
Large spoon

Preparation time: 10 minutes

Baking time: 1 hour

1 Preheat the oven to 375°F.

2 Place the squash on the cutting board. Ask an adult to help you cut each squash in half from top to bottom. Using the soupspoon, scrape out the seeds and strings. Set the squash in the baking pan and put 1 tablespoon butter and 1 tablespoon honey in each half.

3 Cover the pan with aluminum foil and seal the edges by folding the foil around the rim. Put the oven mitts on and place the pan on a rack in the center of the oven. Bake for 1 hour.

4 Put the oven mitts on, slide out the pan, and carefully pull back the aluminum foil, opening the edge that is farthest away from you first, to let the steam escape. Pierce the squash with the fork. If the fork goes in easily, it is done. If the squash is still hard, replace the foil and bake for another 10 minutes. When the squash is ready, put the oven mitts on and place the baking pan on a heatproof surface. Using the large spoon, scoop up each squash half and place it on a plate.

Tabbouleh

Tabbouleh is a wheat grain salad that is popular in the Middle East. The main ingredient, bulgur, may not be available in your local grocery but should be easy to find in a neighborhood health food store. Leftovers taste great scooped up with pita bread or crackers as a tasty after-school snack.

Ingredients

½ cup bulgur wheat
1 cup water
1 ripe medium-size tomato
3 scallions (green onions)
2 bunches fresh parsley sprigs (1½ cups)
2 teaspoons dried mint
3 tablespoons oil
2 tablespoons lemon juice
½ teaspoon salt

Utensils

Measuring cups
Small mixing bowl
Fork
Paper towels
Cutting board
Utility knife
Medium-size mixing bowl
Scissors
Fine-mesh strainer
Measuring spoons
Plastic wrap

Makes: 6 servings

Preparation time: 25 minutes

1 Place the bulgur wheat in the small mixing bowl. Add the water, stir it well with the fork, and let it sit for 20 minutes.

2 Meanwhile, rinse the tomato, pat it dry with paper towels, and place it on the cutting board. Using the utility knife, cut the tomato lengthwise in half. From the top of each tomato half trim a slice that includes the stem and throw the slices away. Cut each half lengthwise into several slices and then cut across the slices several times to make small pieces. Place the tomato pieces in the medium-size mixing bowl.

3 Rinse the scallions, pat them dry with paper towels, and place them on the cutting board. Using the utility knife, trim off the root ends. Slice the scallions up to the dark green leaves. Add the scallions to the tomato in the mixing bowl.

4 Rinse the parsley sprigs and pat them dry with paper towels. Hold the sprigs in a bunch and snip the leafy tops into small pieces with the scissors. You should have 1½ cups. Add the parsley to the other ingredients in the mixing bowl.

5 Place the strainer in the sink and pour in the bulgur to drain. Pat it dry with paper towels and add it to the mixing bowl.

6 Sprinkle the mint over the bulgur. Add the oil, lemon juice, and salt and toss with the fork until mixed. Cover the bowl with plastic wrap and refrigerate for 1 hour or until you are ready to serve.

Rice Casserole

There are hundreds of ways to cook up a rice casserole, but this way, using mixed vegetables, is colorful and makes a tasty side dish for the Chili (page 82) or the Rosemary Chicken (page 84).

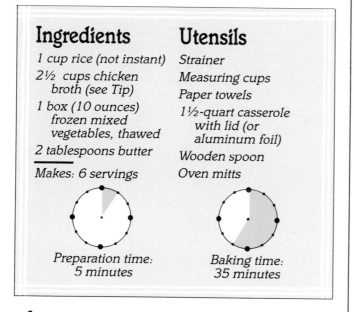

Ingredients

1 cup rice (not instant)

2½ cups chicken broth (see Tip)

1 box (10 ounces) frozen mixed vegetables, thawed

2 tablespoons butter

Makes: 6 servings

Utensils

Strainer

Measuring cups

Paper towels

1½-quart casserole with lid (or aluminum foil)

Wooden spoon

Oven mitts

Preparation time: 5 minutes

Baking time: 35 minutes

1 Preheat the oven to 400°F.

2 Place the strainer in the sink, pour the rice into the strainer, and rinse it under cold running water. Let the rice drain and then pat it dry with paper towels.

3 Pour the rice into the casserole, add the chicken broth and mixed vegetables, and stir it all together.

4 Cover the casserole with a lid or aluminum foil. (Seal the edges of the foil by folding it tightly around the rim.) Put the oven mitts on and place the casserole on a rack in the center of the oven. Bake for 35 minutes.

5 Put the oven mitts on, carefully lift the lid or pull the aluminum foil back, and look to see if the rice has absorbed all the liquid. (If you are using foil, lift the edge that is farthest away from you first, to let the trapped steam escape.) If it hasn't, replace the cover and bake for another 10 minutes. When the rice is ready, put the oven mitts on and place the casserole on a heatproof surface. Take the cover off. Add the butter to the rice and stir with the wooden spoon until the butter is melted. Serve hot.

Tip For the chicken broth you can use either canned chicken broth or 3 chicken bouillon cubes or 3 packets of chicken bouillon diluted in 2½ cups of boiling water.

HAPPY HOLIDAYS

VALENTINE'S DAY

Make these hearts your valentine message. Fancy them up with candy confetti and a personal note written with decorating gel. Give them to all your sweeties, signed from "Guess Who?"

A BEAR'S HEART

Ingredients

5 cups all-purpose flour

1 tablespoon ground ginger

1½ teaspoons baking powder

1 cup solid vegetable shortening

1¾ cups packed brown sugar

3 tablespoons molasses

2 eggs

White Icing (optional; recipe follows)

Candy confetti or jimmies (sprinkles; optional)

Tube of prepared red cake decorating gel (optional)

Makes: Ten 5-inch hearts

Utensils

Measuring cups

Measuring spoons

Medium-size mixing bowl

Fork

Large mixing bowl

Electric mixer

Rubber spatula

Rolling pin

Ruler

Cookie sheets

Waxed paper

5-inch heart-shaped cookie cutter or paper pattern

Small sharp knife (optional)

Oven mitts

Cooling racks

Table knife

Red or white doilies (optional)

Preparation time: 20 minutes

Baking time: 15 minutes

1 Preheat the oven to 350°F.

2 Place 4½ cups of the flour, the ginger, and the baking powder in the medium-size mixing bowl and gently toss together with the fork.

3 Place the shortening and brown sugar in the large mixing bowl. Using the electric mixer, beat at medium speed until the mixture is light brown and fluffy. Stop when necessary to scrape the side of the bowl with the rubber spatula. Add the molasses and beat until blended.

4 Break the eggs into the bowl and mix at medium-low speed until the eggs are completely blended in.

5 Add half the flour mixture and mix at low speed until blended. Add the rest of the flour mixture and mix again.

6 Using some of the remaining ½ cup flour, sprinkle a clean kitchen surface lightly with flour. With your hands, move the dough from the bowl to the floured surface. Shape the dough into a thick circle and sprinkle a little flour over the top. Using the rolling pin, roll the dough until it is about ¼ inch thick (page 8). Measure the dough with a ruler if you are unsure.

7 Line the cookie sheets with waxed paper. Cut the hearts out with the cookie cutter and place them on the cookie sheets. If you are using a paper pattern, place the pattern on the dough and cut around it with the small knife. Stack the scraps on top of each other and press into a thick circle. Roll out the scraps and cut out another heart or two.

8 Put the oven mitts on and place the cookie sheets in the oven. Bake for 15 minutes. Then look to see if the cookies are beginning to brown around the edges. If they are ready, put the oven mitts on and place the cookie sheets on the cooling rack. Let the cookies cool completely.

9 If you want to decorate the cookies, make the icing. Spread the icing on the cookie hearts with the table knife. Sprinkle the candy confetti or jimmies over the still wet icing for extra color and pizazz, or use the red decorating gel to write a message on each cookie. Add a drop or two of the white icing to the center of 10 doilies. Place a cookie on each doily. The icing will help the cookie to stick to the doily. Your special Valentines are now ready.

White Icing

Ingredients
1 egg
2 cups confectioners' sugar
⅛ teaspoon lemon juice

Makes: 1½ cups icing

Utensils
Medium-size mixing bowl
Electric mixer
Measuring cups
Rubber spatula
Measuring spoons
Paper towels

Preparation time: 15 minutes

1 Separate the egg (page 7), letting the egg white fall into the mixing bowl. Save the egg yolk for scrambled eggs or some other use.

2 Using the electric mixer, beat the egg white at high speed until it is frothy and very white. Beat in the sugar, a bit at a time, at medium speed. The icing will get thicker immediately but should remain smooth. Turn off the mixer and clean the side of the bowl with the rubber spatula.

3 Add the lemon juice, which will help the icing to dry once it has been spread on the cookie. Turn the mixer on and beat the icing until you can see the tracks of the beaters when you stop the mixer, about 4 minutes.

4 Wet 3 paper towels under cold running water and squeeze them fairly dry with your hands. Cover the bowl so that the icing will not dry out.

EASTER

This bread bunny is a great decoration for the house at Easter time, and once you get the hang of it, you can use the dough to make all kinds of bread sculptures. Don't eat the bread, though—it's not as tasty as it looks.

BREAD BUNNY

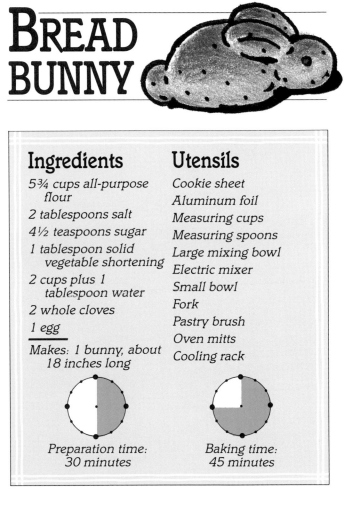

Ingredients

5¾ cups all-purpose flour
2 tablespoons salt
4½ teaspoons sugar
1 tablespoon solid vegetable shortening
2 cups plus 1 tablespoon water
2 whole cloves
1 egg

Makes: 1 bunny, about 18 inches long

Utensils

Cookie sheet
Aluminum foil
Measuring cups
Measuring spoons
Large mixing bowl
Electric mixer
Small bowl
Fork
Pastry brush
Oven mitts
Cooling rack

Preparation time: 30 minutes

Baking time: 45 minutes

1 Line the cookie sheet with aluminum foil.

2 Place 5½ cups of the flour, the salt, sugar, shortening, and 2 cups water in the mixing bowl. Using the electric mixer, mix at low speed until blended.

3 Sprinkle a clean kitchen surface lightly with a little of the remaining flour. Remove the dough from the bowl with your hands and place it on the floured surface. Knead the dough by pushing the dough away from you with the heels of your hands, folding the dough over itself, and turning the dough a quarter turn. Continue kneading until the dough is smooth. If it gets sticky, sprinkle it with a little more flour.

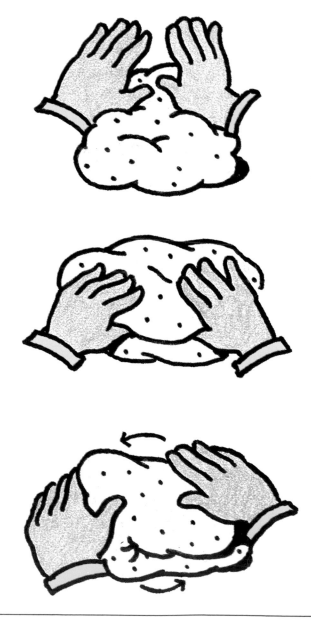

4 Preheat the oven to 400°F.

5 Pull the dough into 2 equal pieces. Shape 1 of the pieces into a smooth ball and place it on the foil-covered cookie sheet. That piece will be the bunny's body.

6 Pull the remaining piece of dough into 3 equal pieces. Shape 1 of the pieces into a smooth ball and place it above the body for the bunny's head. Pinch the head and body together where they meet to connect them.

7 Pull off equal pieces of dough from the remaining 2 pieces and shape them together into a ball about the size of a Ping-Pong ball. Flatten the ball a little and place it next to the body to make the bunny's tail.

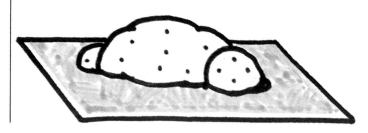

8 Pinch the tail onto the body to connect it. Use your hands to roll the 2 pieces of dough that are left into thick ropes and flatten them out a little so that they look like bunny ears. Place the ears, evenly spaced, on top of the head and pinch the dough together so that they will stick to the head. Push a clove into each side of the head to make the eyes.

9 Break the egg into the small bowl and add the remaining 1 tablespoon water. Use the fork to mix the egg and water until they are completely blended. Brush the bunny with the egg (this will make it golden and shiny when it is baked).

10 Put the oven mitts on and place the cookie sheet in the oven. Bake for 45 minutes. Look to see if the bunny is golden brown. If it is, put the oven mitts on and pull the rack out a little way. Tap the body; if it sounds hollow, the bunny is done. If it's ready, place the cookie sheet on a cooling rack and let the bunny cool for about 20 minutes. Carefully lift the bunny off the cookie sheet with your hands and put it on the cooling rack to cool completely.

Tip If you want the bunny to last a very long time, spray it with lacquer.

FULL-TIME ADULT ASSISTANT NEEDED

HALLOWEEN

These are spooky candy treats for sharing with friends at your school Halloween party. Most stores that sell loose candy sell white chocolate by the pound, so you shouldn't have any problem finding it.

WHITE CHOCOLATE GHOSTS

Ingredients

1 pound white chocolate

Raisins

_____

Makes: 12 ghosts

Preparation time: 30 minutes

Utensils

Cookie sheet

Waxed paper

Double boiler

Pot holder

Cutting board (optional)

Utility knife (optional)

Wooden spoon

Large metal spoon

6 plastic straws, cut in half

1 Line the cookie sheet with waxed paper.

2 Fill the bottom pan of the double boiler half full with water and place it on the stove.

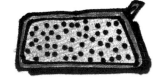

3 Break the chocolate into small pieces with your hands, or if it is too hard, put it on the cutting board and cut it up with the utility knife. Put the chocolate in the top pan of the double boiler.

4 Put the top pan over the bottom pan and turn the heat on to medium. When the chocolate starts to melt, reduce the heat to low. Stir the chocolate with the wooden spoon until half is melted. Stir for another 30 seconds, then remove the top pan from the double boiler and place it on a heat-proof surface. Keep stirring until all the chocolate is melted and smooth.

5 Using the large metal spoon, spread a spoonful of the chocolate on the cookie sheet in the shape of a ghost. It should be ¼ inch thick. Set a straw into the bottom of the ghost, leaving 2 or 3 inches for a handle. Spread more chocolate over the straw and even the shape out if necessary. To make eye holes for your ghosts, press raisins into the chocolate before it hardens.

6 Make 11 more ghosts the same way. If the chocolate begins to harden before you have made all your ghosts, put the pan back over the hot water in the bottom of the double boiler. Stir the chocolate with a kitchen spoon until it has melted, then remove the pan and continue making the ghosts.

7 Let the ghosts cool and harden on the cookie sheet. It will take about 5 minutes, but if you want them to harden faster, you can put the cookie sheet in the freezer. When you're ready to use the ghosts, carefully lift them off the waxed paper.

Tip It's important when working with chocolate to not let it get too hot. It should be about the temperature of your body, which means that if you touch it, it will feel only slightly warm or not warm at all.

THANKSGIVING

FULL-TIME ADULT • ASSISTANT NEEDED •

Imagine the "oohs" and "aahs" as this spectacular soup in its natural serving bowl is brought to the Thanksgiving table! It will be remembered after the turkey is long forgotten.

BAKED PUMPKIN SOUP

Ingredients

1 pumpkin with stem (5 pounds)

1 can (12 ounces) chicken broth

1 can (16 ounces) pumpkin purée

2 cups heavy or whipping cream

½ teaspoon salt

⅛ teaspoon white pepper

Pinch ground mace

Pinch ground nutmeg

Makes: 4 to 6 servings

Utensils

Newspaper

Utility knife

Large metal spoon

Cookie sheet

Can opener

Large mixing bowl

Whisk

Measuring cups

Measuring spoons

Oven mitts

Wide spatula

Ladle

Preparation time: 35 minutes

Baking time: 40 minutes

1 Spread several full sheets of the newspaper on a working surface and put the pumpkin on the newspaper. Ask an adult to help you cut a 4-inch-wide circle around the stem of the pumpkin.

6 Ask an adult to help you put the cookie sheet in the oven. Bake for 40 minutes. Then look to see if the pumpkin has softened. Test it by piercing the top with the utility knife. Don't pierce the side of the pumpkin. (You may want an adult to help do this.) If the pumpkin isn't soft, bake it for another 10 minutes but make sure the pumpkin doesn't get so soft that it can't hold the soup.

7 When it is ready, put the oven mitts on and get an adult to help you put the cookie sheet on a heat-proof surface. Slide the spatula under the pumpkin and lift it onto a serving platter.

2 Take the top off and scrape the seeds and strings out of the pumpkin, first with your hands and then by scraping it clean with the large spoon.

3 Place the pumpkin on the cookie sheet. Roll up the newspaper and throw it away.

4 Preheat the oven to 375°F.

5 Open the cans of chicken broth and pumpkin purée with the can opener and pour them into the mixing bowl. Using the whisk, mix the two together. Add the cream and whisk again. Then add the salt, pepper, mace, and nutmeg and whisk again until blended. Pour the pumpkin mixture into the pumpkin and put the lid on.

8 Insert the utility knife between the lid and the pumpkin and press down to lift the lid up. The steam may have sealed the lid tightly, so you may have to insert the knife around the lid at several places. When the lid is loose enough to lift, do it carefully. The steam coming up from the soup will be very hot, so don't have your face too close.

9 As soon as the lid is off, serve the soup, scraping some of the baked pumpkin from the inside of the shell with each ladle of soup.

CHRISTMAS

These cookie-cards make delicious Christmas tree decorations for all your friends. Maybe each friend should get two—one for their tree and one for their tummy. Because the dough for these cookies is prepared the same way you prepare the dough for A Bear's Heart, you will be using the ingredients and utensils listed on page 98. The additional ingredients and utensils are listed below.

GINGERBREAD CHRISTMAS CARDS

Ingredients

In addition to the ingredients on page 98 you will need:

White Icing (recipe on page 100)

Tiny candy canes (optional)

Red and white–striped peppermint drops (optional)

Red and green gumdrops (optional)

Makes: Approximately ten 5-inch cookies

Utensils

In addition to the utensils on page 98 you will need:

Star-shaped and Christmas-tree-shaped cookie cutters (you will not need the heart-shaped cookie cutter)

Vegetable peeler

Scissors

Thin Christmas ribbon

Preparation time: 20 minutes

Baking time: 15 minutes

1 Make the Bear's Heart cookie dough through step 5.

2 Preheat the oven to 400°F.

3 Line the cookie sheets with waxed paper.

4 Roll the dough out as directed in step 6 for making the bears' hearts. Using a table knife, cut the dough into card-shaped rectangles or squares or Christmas ball designs like circles and triangles. Use the cookie cutters to make trees and stars. Using the vegetable peeler, make a hole near the top of each of the cookies, and then put them on the cookie sheets.

5 Put the oven mitts on and put the cookie sheets in the oven. Bake for 15 minutes. Look to see if the edges of the cookies are beginning to turn brown. If they are not ready, bake for another 3 minutes and check again.

6 When the cookies are baked, put the oven mitts on and place the cookie sheets on cooling racks. Let the cookies cool for about 10 minutes and then use a spatula to move the cookies to a clean kitchen counter.

7 Make the White Icing. Use it to decorate the cookies with Christmas designs and messages. If you want, you can add the following candies to the still wet icing: tiny candy canes, red and white–striped peppermint drops, slices of red and green gumdrops, or any other favorite traditional Christmas candy.

8 Use the scissors to cut a long piece of ribbon for each cookie. String a piece through the hole in each cookie, tie the ribbon in a bow, and your card is ready to hang on a Christmas tree.

HANUKKAH

Latkes, potato pancakes, are traditionally served as a dinner side dish during the Jewish holiday of Hanukkah. Fry these up nice and crispy and accompany them with a bowl of applesauce.

GRANDMA'S POTATO LATKES

Ingredients

7 medium-size potatoes, preferably baking potatoes
1 small onion
2 eggs
¼ cup all-purpose flour
2 teaspoons salt
½ teaspoon pepper
3 cups vegetable oil
Applesauce

Makes: 8 pancakes

Utensils

2 large mixing bowls
Vegetable peeler
Cutting board
Utility knife
Grater
Wooden spoon
Measuring cups
Measuring spoons
Large strainer
Medium-size mixing bowl
Paper towels
Waxed paper
Ovenproof plate
10-inch frying pan
Pot holder
Spatula
Oven mitts

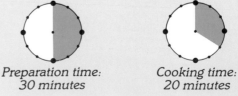

Preparation time: 30 minutes

Cooking time: 20 minutes

1 Put 1 large mixing bowl in the sink and fill it with cold water. Using the peeler, peel the potatoes and put the potatoes in the bowl of cold water.

2 Put the onion on the cutting board. Using the utility knife, trim off the ends. Peel the skin off the onion, and throw it away along with the ends. Put the grater in the other large mixing bowl and, using the largest holes on the grater, carefully grate the onion into the bowl. (Do this slowly so that you don't scrape your knuckles.)

3 Break the eggs into the bowl and mix them with the onion, using the wooden spoon. Add the flour, salt, and pepper and mix thoroughly.

4 Place the strainer over the medium-size mixing bowl. Take one of the potatoes out of the water and dry it with a paper towel. Using the largest holes on the grater, carefully grate the potato over a sheet of waxed paper and then put the grated potato in the strainer to drain. Grate the remaining potatoes, one at a time, in the same way, remembering to go slowly and watch your knuckles.

5 When all the potatoes are grated and in the strainer, press down on them to squeeze out as much liquid as possible. Then add the potatoes to the egg mixture and stir it all together.

6 Preheat the oven to 200°F. Line the ovenproof plate with a few layers of paper towels.

7 Ask an adult to help you fry the latkes. Put the frying pan on the stove and pour enough oil into the pan to measure ¼ inch. Heat the oil over medium heat until it begins to spatter (stay back a little way so that none gets on you). Measure ⅓ cup of the potato mixture and pour it into the skillet. Gently flatten it with the spatula and fry the potato pancake until the bottom is crisp and brown, 2 to 3 minutes. Using the spatula, carefully flip the pancake over and fry the second side until it browns, about 2 more minutes.

8 Use the spatula to take the pancake out of the skillet and put it to drain on the paper-towel-covered ovenproof plate. Put the plate in the oven to keep the pancake warm while you fry the remaining pancakes. Add more oil to the frying pan as it is needed, remembering to stand back from the stove so that the oil doesn't splatter on you as it hits the hot pan. As each pancake is cooked, add it to the plate in the oven. As soon as the last pancake is done, using your oven mitts, take the plate out of the oven and serve the pancakes accompanied by a bowl of applesauce.

DESSERT

Chunky Chocolate-Chip Bears

The success of these cookies doesn't depend on your getting them to look like Teddy Bears. Like the Teddy Bear Pancakes (page 12), they'll taste great in whatever shape you create.

Ingredients

2½ cups all-purpose flour

½ teaspoon baking soda

1 cup (2 sticks) butter, at room temperature

¼ cup solid vegetable shortening

½ cup granulated sugar

⅓ cup packed dark brown sugar

1 egg

1 teaspoon vanilla extract

2 cups semisweet chocolate chips

1 cup chopped walnuts

Makes: 24 bear-shaped cookies

Preparation time: 30 minutes

Baking time: 10 minutes

Utensils

2 cookie sheets

Aluminum foil

Measuring cups

Measuring spoons

Medium-size mixing bowl

Fork

Large mixing bowl

Electric mixer

Rubber spatula

Teaspoon

Oven mitts

Spatula

1 Preheat the oven to 350°F.

2 Line the cookie sheets with aluminum foil.

3 Place the flour and baking soda in the medium-size bowl and mix it with the fork.

4 Place the butter, shortening, and granulated and brown sugars in the large mixing bowl. Using the electric mixer, mix for 2 minutes on medium speed. Turn the mixer off and, using the rubber spatula, clean the side of the bowl. Mix again until the sugar and butter are completely blended, about 2 more minutes.

5 Break the egg into the bowl and add the vanilla. Mix at medium speed for 1 minute. Turn the mixer off and scrape the side of the bowl clean.

6 Add about half the flour mixture and mix at low speed until blended. Add the remaining flour mixture and mix until blended again.

7 Add the chocolate chips and walnuts and mix at the lowest speed until they are scattered evenly throughout the dough.

8 To make the Teddy Bear shapes, scoop up a mound of dough with the teaspoon and drop it onto a cookie sheet. This dough will make the bear's body. Scoop up a small bit of dough on the tip of the spoon for the head and drop it above the body. Then place 4 small mounds next to the body for the arms and legs. Using your fingers, gently press the body flat and make sure the head and arms and legs are close to the body. Make more Teddy Bears about 2 inches apart on the cookie sheets.

9 Put the oven mitts on and place the cookie sheets in the oven. Bake until the edges of the cookies begin to turn brown, 10 to 12 minutes.

10 Put the oven mitts on and remove the cookie sheets from the oven to a heatproof surface. Let the cookies cool completely. Gently remove the cookies with the metal spatula.

Tip If you keep the cookies in airtight containers, they will stay fresh for a week.

Brownies

Short, fat, fudgy, chewy, chunky Brownies that go great with a tall, skinny glass of cold milk!

Ingredients

4 ounces unsweetened baking chocolate

½ cup (1 stick) butter

1½ teaspoons butter, at room temperature

3 eggs

1½ cups sugar

1 teaspoon vanilla extract

1 cup all-purpose flour

1 cup chopped walnuts

Makes: 18 brownies

Preparation time: 20 minutes

Baking time: 30 minutes

Utensils

Double boiler

Pot holder

Wooden spoon

Measuring spoons

12 x 8-inch baking pan

Paper towels

Large mixing bowl

Measuring cups

Electric mixer

Rubber spatula

Oven mitts

Utility knife

1 Fill the bottom pan of the double boiler half full with water. Place the pan on the stove and heat over medium heat to a simmer. Break the chocolate into big pieces with your hands and place them in the top pan of the double boiler. Add ½ cup butter to the chocolate and fit the pan in the bottom of the double boiler. Reduce the heat to low and melt the chocolate and butter, stirring occasionally with the wooden spoon. When both are completely melted, remove the top pan and set it on a heatproof surface to cool.

2 Preheat the oven to 325°F.

3 Spread 1 ½ teaspoons butter on the bottom and sides of the baking pan with a paper towel.

4 Break the eggs into the mixing bowl. Add the sugar and vanilla. Using the electric mixer, beat until the mixture is light and creamy, 2 to 3 minutes.

5 Add the chocolate mixture, scraping the pan clean with the rubber spatula, and mix at low speed for 1 minute. Turn the mixer off and scrape the side of the bowl clean. Mix for another minute and then turn the mixer off and add half the flour. Mix at low speed until the flour is mixed in. Add the remaining flour and the walnuts and mix until blended.

6 Pour the batter into the buttered baking pan, scraping the bowl clean with the spatula. Put the oven mitts on and place the pan on a rack in the center of the oven. Bake for 30 minutes.

7 Put the oven mitts on and remove the pan from the oven to a heat-proof surface. Let the brownies cool for 15 minutes before cutting.

8 Using the utility knife, cut the brownies lengthwise into 3 even strips and then cut across the strips every 2 inches.

Tip Wrap any brownies that aren't eaten right away in pieces of plastic wrap. They will stay fresh for several days.

Beehive Cupcakes

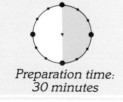

The chocolate jimmies sprinkled on the mounded, swirled icing make these cupcakes really look like beehives.

Ingredients

2½ cups all-purpose flour

1 tablespoon cornstarch

1 tablespoon baking powder

¼ teaspoon ground cloves

½ cup (1 stick) butter, at room temperature

1½ cups sugar

4 eggs

1 cup milk

¾ cup miniature chocolate chips

Beehive Frosting (recipe follows)

¼ cup chocolate jimmies (sprinkles) as decoration

Makes: 18 cupcakes

Utensils

18 paper cupcake liners

2 muffin tins

Measuring cups

Measuring spoons

2 large mixing bowls

Fork

Electric mixer

Rubber spatula

Small ladle

Oven mitts

Cooling rack

Table knife

Preparation time: 30 minutes

Baking time: 20 minutes

1 Preheat the oven to 375°F.

2 Put the paper liners in 18 muffin cups.

3 Place the flour, cornstarch, baking powder, and cloves in one of the mixing bowls and mix with the fork.

4 Place the butter and sugar in the other mixing bowl. Using the electric mixer, beat at medium-high speed until the mixture is light and creamy, 3 to 4 minutes. Turn the mixer off and clean the side of the bowl with the rubber spatula when necessary.

5 Break 1 of the eggs into the bowl with the butter mixture and beat until the egg is thoroughly mixed in. Beat in the remaining 3 eggs, one at a time. The mixture will be quite runny.

6 Add half the flour mixture and mix at medium speed until blended. Add half the milk and mix again until blended. Mix in the remaining flour mixture and then the remaining milk. To make this easier, you can turn off the mixer while you are adding each new ingredient.

7 Add the chocolate chips and mix at the lowest speed until the chips are scattered evenly through the batter. Scrape the side of the bowl clean.

8 Using the small ladle, spoon the batter into the muffin cups, dividing the batter evenly.

9 Put the oven mitts on and put the muffin tins in the oven. Bake until the tops are golden brown, about 20 minutes. (Now is the time to make the frosting.)

10 Put the oven mitts on and remove the tins from the oven to the cooling rack. Let the cupcakes cool in the tin for about 5 minutes and then, wearing the mitts, turn the pan upside down and let the cupcakes fall onto the cooling rack. Turn the cupcakes right side up and let them cool completely before frosting.

11 Using the table knife, spread the frosting in hive-shaped, swirled mounds on the cupcakes and then sprinkle the jimmies over the frosting.

Beehive Frosting

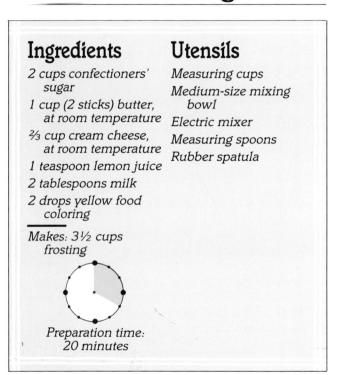

Ingredients

2 cups confectioners' sugar

1 cup (2 sticks) butter, at room temperature

⅔ cup cream cheese, at room temperature

1 teaspoon lemon juice

2 tablespoons milk

2 drops yellow food coloring

Makes: 3½ cups frosting

Preparation time: 20 minutes

Utensils

Measuring cups

Medium-size mixing bowl

Electric mixer

Measuring spoons

Rubber spatula

1 While the cupcakes are cooling, make the frosting: Place the confectioners' sugar, butter, and cream cheese in the mixing bowl. Using the electric mixer, mix at medium speed until the mixture is smooth and creamy.

2 Add the lemon juice and beat at medium-high speed for 1 minute. Clean the side of the bowl with the rubber spatula.

3 Add the milk and yellow food coloring and beat until completely blended, 30 seconds to 1 minute.

Chocolate Wafer Parfait

You can make this layered dessert using any favorite crispy cookies. In fact, you can even use chewy ones like crumbled Chunky Chocolate-Chip Bears (page 114).

1 Pour the cream and vanilla into the mixing bowl. Using the electric mixer, beat the cream at medium speed until it is thick and fluffy, about 2½ minutes.

2 Layer the cookies and cream in 4 parfait or wine glasses by heaping 1 teaspoonful of whipped cream into each glass and then adding 1 cookie. Add another teaspoon of cream and another cookie until the cream and the cookies are all in the glasses.

Ingredients

1 cup heavy or whipping cream

½ teaspoon vanilla extract

40 chocolate wafers or other thin crisp cookies

Makes: 4 parfaits

Preparation time: 10 minutes

Utensils

Measuring cups

Measuring spoons

Mixing bowl

Electric mixer

Teaspoon

Plastic wrap

Chilling time: 2½ hours

3 Cover the tops of the glasses with plastic wrap and refrigerate 2½ hours before serving.

Strawberries and Cream

You can really tell that spring has arrived when plump rosy strawberries appear in the local market. They only need a touch of cream to make a perfect dessert.

Ingredients

1 pint strawberries
½ cup heavy or whipping cream
1 teaspoon sugar
¼ teaspoon vanilla extract

Makes: 4 servings

Utensils

Strainer
Measuring cups
Medium-size mixing bowl
Measuring spoons
Electric mixer
Paper towels
Soupspoon

Preparation time: 10 minutes

1 Place the strainer in the sink. Pull any green leaves off the strawberries. Place the strawberries in the strainer, rinse quickly under cold running water, and let them drain.

2 Pour the cream into the mixing bowl. Add the sugar and vanilla. Using the electric mixer, beat the cream at medium-high speed until it is thick and fluffy.

3 Gently pat the strawberries dry with paper towels and divide the berries among 4 dessert bowls. Spoon the whipped cream over the berries and serve.

Frozen Strawberry Soufflés

A t the end of a spectacular meal, bring out these extra-special soufflés (see Tip). They are easy to make, but be sure to prepare them far enough ahead so they have plenty of time to harden.

Ingredients

2 tablespoons butter, at room temperature

1 pint strawberries

¾ cup sugar

2 cups heavy or whipping cream, cold

5 eggs, at room temperature

Makes: 4 individual soufflés

Utensils

Scissors

Aluminum foil

Paper towels

Five 4-ounce plastic or paper cups

3 mixing bowls

Measuring cups

Electric mixer

Rubber spatula

Preparation time: 20 minutes

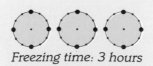

Freezing time: 3 hours

1 Cut 4 strips of aluminum foil long enough to wrap around each of 4 of the cups.

2 Using a paper towel, lightly spread some butter on each strip of aluminum foil. With the buttered side of the foil against the cup, wrap the strip around the cup, leaving a foil rim about 1½ inches high above the cup. The butter will make the foil strips stick to the cups. Freeze the 4 cups while you make the soufflé mixture. Put the extra cup aside for now.

3 Pull off any green leaves from the strawberries, then quickly rinse them under cold running water. Pat them dry with paper towels and place them in one of the mixing bowls. Add ¼ cup of the sugar to the bowl. Using the electric mixer, crush the berries at the lowest speed until they are in small chunks. Wash, then dry, the beaters.

4 Pour the heavy cream into another bowl and beat it with the electric mixer until it is thick and fluffy. When you turn the mixer off and pull the beaters out of the cream, the cream should be pulled up in a peak. Wait a few seconds to see if the peak falls. If it does, beat the cream a little longer and check again. Place the bowl in the refrigerator. Wash, then dry, the beaters.

5 Break the eggs into the last mixing bowl and add the remaining ½ cup sugar. Using the mixer, beat the eggs at high speed until they are pale yellow and light. When you turn the mixer off and lift the beater, the mixture should fall in a ribbon on top of the mixture in the bowl.

6 Add the strawberries to the egg mixture and gently stir them in with the rubber spatula. Take the whipped cream out of the refrigerator and gently blend it into the eggs and strawberries.

7 Remove the cups from the freezer and place them next to the bowl with the soufflé mix. Using the fifth cup, scoop up the soufflé mixture and pour it into the foil-rimmed cups. Fill the cups almost to the top of the foil strips. Place the cups in the freezer and freeze for 3 hours.

8 When you are ready to serve the soufflés, take the aluminum foil strips off the cups.

Tip This recipe uses raw eggs. Recently uncooked eggs have been the source of salmonella, a serious infection. If you are unsure of the quality of the eggs you buy, don't make this recipe.

Did You Know?
The English put together the largest bowl of strawberries ever— it weighed 451 pounds. Now that's a lot of berries!

Apple Pizzas

FULL-TIME ADULT ASSISTANT NEEDED

Usually pizzas bring to mind saucy toppings and gooey cheese. Here's an all-American apple pie twist to serve at dessert time with each person getting his or her own.

Ingredients

2 ¼ cups all-purpose flour

10 tablespoons (1 ¼ sticks) butter, at room temperature

3 tablespoons plus 1 teaspoon sugar

¼ teaspoon salt

¼ cup cold water

3 medium-size apples

½ teaspoon cinnamon

Makes: Four 6-inch pizzas

Utensils

Measuring cups

Large mixing bowl

Measuring spoons

Rolling pin

Ruler

6-inch-wide plate or bowl

Utility knife

Spatula

Cookie sheet

Cutting board

Apple corer

Vegetable peeler

Medium-size mixing bowl

Oven mitts

Preparation time: 40 minutes

Baking time: 15 minutes

1 Preheat the oven to 400°F.

2 Place the flour and butter in the large mixing bowl. Using your fingers, rub the butter into the flour until the butter disappears and the flour looks a little yellow.

3 Add 3 tablespoons sugar and the salt to the flour and blend it all together with your hands. Pour in the cold water and blend with your hands until the dough holds together in one clump. Sprinkle a clean surface with a little extra flour and place the dough on the surface.

4 To knead, first press the dough flat with your fingers. Place the heels of your hands on the dough, press them down, and push the dough away from you. Curl your fingers over the far edge of the dough and fold it back over itself. Turn the dough a quarter turn. Push and then fold the dough in half again. Continue to turn, push, and fold the dough for 5 minutes. If the dough starts to stick, sprinkle a little more flour under and over it. Shape the dough into a ball.

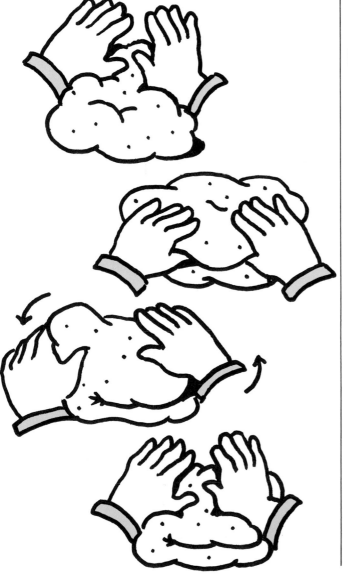

5 Divide the dough into 4 equal pieces. Using the rolling pin, roll out one piece about ¼ inch thick (page 8). Use a ruler to measure if you aren't sure. Sprinkle the dough with a little more flour to keep it from sticking to the rolling pin when you roll it out.

Turn the 6-inch-wide plate or bowl upside down onto the dough, and use the plate as a guide to cut away the excess dough with the utility knife. Remove the plate, slide the spatula under the circle of dough, and place it on the cookie sheet. Roll out and cut the other pieces of dough the same way.

6 Place the apples on the cutting board. Push the apple corer through the center of each apple and twist out the core. Peel the apples with the peeler. Cut the apples in half with the utility knife. Turn the halves flat side down onto the cutting board and cut each half into 7 or 8 slices. Put the apple slices in the medium-size mixing bowl. Sprinkle them with 1 teaspoon sugar and the cinnamon and toss the apples in the bowl to distribute the sugar and cinnamon.

7 Arrange apple slices on each circle of dough with the slices overlapping in a circle.

8 Put the oven mitts on and place the cookie sheet in the oven. Bake for 15 minutes. Then look to see if the edge of the crust is golden brown. If the pizzas are ready, put the oven mitts on and remove the cookie sheet from the oven to a heatproof surface. Slip the spatula under each pizza and transfer it to a plate. The pizzas are terrific hot out of the oven or cooled to room temperature.

Tip You can make the dough and roll it out ahead of time. Keep it in the refrigerator, covered, until you are ready to add the apples and bake.

Did You Know?

The longest piece ever peeled from one apple was 172 feet 4 inches before it broke. The apple weighed 20 ounces.

Index